Joyful Productivity for Solopreneurs

Gentle Practices for Consistent Creativity, Wellbeing and Deep Meaning in Work

George Kao

Authentic Business Coach

www.GeorgeKao.com

Praise from readers of the 1st Edition:

"The beauty and inspiration offered by this book is exactly on how I can create structure in my daily work life, in ways that can be inspiring."

–Ruth Toledo Altschuler

"Every productivity issue I have personally struggled with as a solo business owner, is addressed in this beautiful book full of heart, in ways that feel loving, kind and authentic to me."

–Liesel Teversham

" I finished the book feeling much more optimistic about the possibility of working in a more satisfying and productive way and will be going back through it to find more tools that I can try out."

–Roshan Daryanani

"As a business owner, being productive is one thing, but being joyful at the same time has proved to be more challenging as my business has grown. I have already started using the tools here, and I will keep this book close at hand to continue to challenge myself to keep the balance and joy in my life. This book is a wellspring of hope for those who are struggling to get things done."

–Tracy Gimpel

"I have been a fan of George Kao's work for years and this book packages his wisdom, heart, and expertise in a way that anyone can begin implementing today. Personally, I will be adding this book to the resources on my website and I will be suggesting it to clients as it is a way to reduce stress and bring them back into the present which is the only place we can get anything done."

–Gina Ryan

"For the 1st time in years my email is up-to-date and the desktop on my computer is all in one folder so that when I open it the screen is just my background picture. I can't tell you how those simple things have made my life easier. I highly recommend the book Joyful Productivity! Implementing just a few manageable little steps is changing my business life!"

–Michelle Wolff

It's important to me that these ideas get out into the world and implemented, so that more people can work with more joyful productivity.

–George Kao

Contents

A Note for Paperback Readers

Throughout, there are words and phrases that will be clickable in the digital copy of the book.

You can purchase the digital copy via Amazon for a lower price than the paperback.

If you dont mind reading a web-based version, you can view the whole digital book, complete with links, here – www.bit.ly/joyfulprobook2022 – all lower case.

Please keep the link private, as its only for those who have bought (or borrowed) the book.

Thank you, and enjoy the book!

George Kao

Foreword by Taylor Jacobson

It was another bright, dusty day in Pune, India. I was nestled into a familiar groove on the couch — computer overheating on my lap, fan raging overhead — engrossed in my latest entrepreneurial hustle, when my phone rang.

I answered, and my girlfriend's voice came pouring out, half-cry, half-shout — something about a car crash.

"Are you okay?" I asked.

She was okay, she said.

She started explaining what happened, but I had already checked out... *She's got this under control*, I said to myself. We hung up the phone, and I turned my attention back to my computer.

Had I truly listened, I might have heard the shock, the cry for support. I would have done the caring thing and driven the 15 minutes to meet her.

But with a deadline looming, I was stressed out and numbed out.

I had been glued to the couch for days on end. My eyes were aching and bloodshot. My lower back was protesting violently.

If she had said that aliens were invading, I'm not sure I'd have been roused from my state.

My now-ex was indeed okay (and has since forgiven me), but my ambition and anxiety had squeezed the patience, compassion, and presence out of me.

A few months later, my fledgling startup folded. In spite of my best efforts, and the cost to my health and relationships, I had failed.

In the seven years between that conversation and this writing, neither my ambition nor my quest for productivity have waned. But in the wake of that episode, I realized there had to be a better way.

I started studying productivity and testing new methods—first in my life, later as an executive coach, today as CEO of a behavioral technology company dedicated to helping people do their best work, through the power of community and accountability. That path led me to George Kao, and to many of the techniques you will find in this book.

I discovered that truly productive people excel not by working more, but by applying their time and energy toward creative, original, and valuable work. They prioritize, choosing to move "big rocks", while resisting the urge to put out every fire. They ground themselves, so that their work is an expression of intention and inner truth—not one of fear and anxiety and reactivity.

For instance, did you know that the optimally productive number of working hours, according to research, is 35 hours per week? While you may be exceptional, the reality is we're all human. Past 35 hours, most people simply cannot sustain the wellbeing required to do great work and make hard choices. But should one's goal really be "optimal productivity" anyway?

What if our work contributed to our wellbeing, rather than detracting from it?

You will find no better teacher of mindful productivity than George Kao. With this book, *Joyful Productivity*, George has not only assembled his best lessons to boost your output, but also provided a roadmap to experience more presence, flow, and authentic self-expression in your work and life.

Today, not only do I work fewer hours, I do other strange things too—things like sleeping 9 hours per night, reading quietly in the morning, taking a daily midday stroll in the park, even getting the occasional massage-in-the-middle-of-the-workday (which I did on Wednesday this week). I've never been more productive, and my loved ones don't mind the change either!

In a world that values busyness over reflection, where we're bombarded by distractions, mindful focus is an increasingly crucial skill. Focus can separate success from failure, serenity from anxiety, and the satisfaction of sharing your gifts with the world from the regret of procrastination.

So grab a nourishing beverage, find a comfortable spot, and spend some time with this valuable book—you are in for a treat. Just make sure you slow down enough to absorb and enjoy it!!

Taylor Jacobson
Founder & CEO, Focusmate

1. Do Your Work from an Inner Spark of Joy

The only thing you control at work is your state of being.

How are you being, as you go about your tasks and your work?

Are you anxious, struggling, and just wanting to get it done?

The quality of your work tends to match the quality of your being.

You have no guarantees of your results – you can only control how you do the work. Therefore, why not work from joy... instead of anxiety, boredom, or frustration?

Your state of being is your top priority, because the only thing you truly can control is your inner life.

—

The quality of your life arises from *the quality of your being.*

The quality of your being arises from *the quality of your daily practice.*

Today, practice tapping into the spark of joy within you.

From there, do your work.

—

If we want some level of material comfort, or the experience of achievement, growth, and fulfillment, we cannot escape work.

Since work **must** be done, the only thing left in your control is **how** you do the work.

You are working towards a better future: for your life, for your family, and for the world. Yet, you have no guarantee that your work today will contribute to that.

What you can control for sure is **how you feel** as you do your work.

The truth is that **you are always practicing** how you do your work.

Most of us are never taught how to practice well. We're only taught to "work hard." We imagine hard work to be something like having a slight scowl on our face, tense shoulders, short shallow breaths, and inner struggle.

"Hustle!" "Grind!"

That is what many people have been practicing for years.

No wonder so many of us yearn for easy money, easy work, easy life, even though we know those to be shallow illusions that don't truly add value to our growth.

We need to do real work, deep work, to really advance our vision for the world and our own lives. There are real problems that are deeply calling to us, crying out for our best contribution.

Yet, we are afraid because we have been practicing the idea of "working hard" (as inner suffering) all our lives, and so we resist it.

It's no wonder that we wish to avoid "work" as we know it to be.

—

The more we practice something, the more natural it becomes.

Because you have always experienced work as anxiety, stress, frustration, or boredom, it may feel more natural that way.

But for *any* task, you can learn to practice a different way.

—

Throughout the day, in any moment of negativity – when you experience anxiety, stress, confusion, tension, or boredom – any moment when you don't feel joy, peace, or love... it is because you have temporarily forgotten the Spark.

The Spark within you can never be extinguished. It goes by various names: Consciousness, Higher Self, Spirit, Your True Nature, Inner Peace, Joy, Love, the Force, God.

The Spark is always, patiently, waiting for you to reconnect.

Whenever you tap into the Spark, you feel a deep sense of joy, peace, love. When you practice tapping into the Spark on a regular basis (ideally, many times in a day) those good feelings start to pervade your entire life... including how you work.

No matter what is happening, no matter the decisions you've made, no matter the mistakes or failures, the Spark is always with you, patiently available, ready to be kindled into a warm fire.

Yet, it only comes with practice. Tapping into the Spark is *a skill* you can learn, and with enough repetition, it becomes natural.

One of the core practices for me to reconnect with my Spark is the Energy Reboot. I do this many times a day, as frequently as every 15 minutes during a working hour. The practice only takes 30 seconds. It works well as a microbreak.

Other practices people may find useful include: mindfulness meditation, prayer, spiritual music, dance, or any activity that allows you to feel the joy, peace, and love of the Spark.

But don't just do it in the morning or evening! Do *it every hour during your working day*. It is a wonderful way to build the practice of **deep joy**, making it a habit that pervades your entire day.

(If it's hard for you to feel the Spark, it can be very helpful to use the services of a spiritual mentor, counselor, or coach. Feel free to reach out to me for recommendations.)

When you are connected with your Spark, you feel a deep sense of well-being.

To build an authentic business, the top priority for any work session is to first access that state of deep well-being. Then from there, do your work. You will enjoy your work so much more. Others will more likely enjoy your work, too.

Whatever the results, people will appreciate **the way** you do your work.

And how you do your work will also remind them of *their* Spark. You will be adding deep value to others... truly bettering the world.

Instead of trying to manipulate the world to your vision before you can be happy, first connect with the Spark to get into the state of deep happiness. From that inner state, do the work that *might* contribute externally to a better life and world.

We often sacrifice our journey for our results. But what if the journey is as important as our results?

Regardless of outer results, for which we have no guarantee, if you practice connecting with the Spark, you will always experience a rich and joyful inner life.

—

The real challenge for staying connected to your Spark is when you need to respond to a difficult situation or person.

Most of us have practiced years of responding from our ego, reflecting our view of what the world and others *should* be like. We are trying to have things our way.

It may feel natural to operate from ego and feel negativity when things don't go according to our preference, but it doesn't have to be this way. What's natural is what's repeated. You can change that nature.

From now on, take a few deep breaths, and practice tapping into your Spark, before responding to the challenging situation or person.

If we are always trying to manipulate the world and others to suit our vision, life becomes an endless struggle. We do not need to force our idea of what *should* happen before we allow ourselves to be happy.

Instead, when we practice tapping into the Spark first, we can experience the peace, the joy, the love that is always within us, always awaiting our reconnection. Life becomes bliss.

Today, and in any moment, you are either practicing ego and negativity, or you are practicing tapping into your Spark.

You always have a choice.

I wish you a life and work that arises from a deep sense of well-being.

To watch the companion video or comment on this chapter, go here: www.bit.ly/jpv2c1

2. Focus on Systems Every Day, not Goals

In entrepreneurship, we often encounter a fixation on big goals and dramatic results.

"Get 1 million followers!"

"Build a 7-figure business!"

When that is the constant focus, two things happen:

1. Your subconscious keeps telling you—daily—that you aren't there... that you aren't yet "enough."

"Desire is a contract that you make with yourself to be unhappy until you get what you want." *–Naval Ravikant*

The fixation on a big numeric goal (such as "7 figure income" or "1 million followers") creates an underlying layer of unhappiness or anxiety with one's current life.

2. The more you focus on the specifics of the goal, the more you become attached to how it must turn out.

If the end result doesn't happen in the way you visualized, or following the timeline you expected, it can deal a blow to your self-esteem, and erode your sense of self-empowerment.

I prefer to look at goals in a different, perhaps healthier way:

I focus on my systems—my daily processes—rather than my goals.

(Ironically, I've found that, over time, this tends to create better results, too!)

I'm not saying to get rid of goals.

I, too, have a vision for my future life and specific milestones I aim for.

But I hold loosely to those future numbers and milestones. I think of them as *potentials* rather than as a rigid definition of success.

I use a future vision to help me **design a daily system** that will move me toward the vision, turning possibilities into **probabilities**.

The farther out the goal, the less we can accurately predict when (or even if!) we will achieve it.

When it comes to whether I will reach my milestones, I know that there are too many uncontrollable factors: personal circumstances I can't foresee, technological and market changes that will surprise everyone, and other future revelations that may require a big change in direction.

So let's be careful not to get fixated on a future goal that we made up.

Instead, let's create a system for action that makes it more likely that the goal will become reality.

Simple examples:

Goal = Write a book.
System = Write 1 page per day.

Goal = Get 5 more clients.
System = Contact 5 people per week.

Goal = Earn $3,000 in passive income.
System = Create 1 new online course every 60 days.

If the system feels daunting to you, then specify smaller, more doable steps, in order to prevent procrastination. Examples:

System: Contact 5 people a week.

Doable steps:

1. Schedule a <u>Focusmate</u> session for taking the following actions.
2. Write the names of 10 people I might contact this week.
3. Narrow that list down to five people I'm energized to reach out to.
4. Look at each of their social media to take a note about how I can start my note to them.
5. Write and send a note to each of them.

If you apply your system consistently, and observe your results, you'll find clarity on how to make *the system* better, thereby increasing the probability of reaching your goal!

Creating the system—the process of daily or weekly actions—is the first major step.

We can then take the next step to make it more meaningful. We can elevate our purpose for that system: **to grow our skills and capacity.**

In other words, we are now reframing the ultimate motive for the system from "reaching the goal" to "improving ourselves."

Why? Because the only "goal" that truly matters is our growth.

As long as you are developing your abilities and character, you are becoming more valuable to society. And if you keep doing that, then Life will become progressively more joyful and meaningful for you.

Any goal instantly becomes more purposeful when you connect it to the deeper goal of *growing yourself.*

Interestingly, when we focus on our systems—rather than our goals—we also tend to experience better results.

Here's a wonderful little story from the book The Practicing Mind:

"I once read an interview with a coach for the U.S. Olympic archery team. He commented that the biggest problem he faced in coaching the American team was that they were fixated on their scores, or the result of their shots.

It was as if they were drawing the bow and releasing the arrow only to hit the bull's-eye and earn a good score.

This was in contrast to the Asian teams, who, having grown up in different cultures, were consumed in the process of properly executing the technique that led up to releasing the shot. Where the arrow hit the target was almost unimportant compared to the motion of drawing the bow correctly and releasing the shot.

They viewed the result with an almost detached indifference. For them, the desired goal was a natural result of prioritizing the proper technique of drawing the bow. They operated in a completely different paradigm, and because of it, they were very difficult to beat.... The minds of the Asian archers were quiet, uncomplicated, and free from mental turmoil.

The irony was that, when compared to the results-oriented Americans, the Asians were the ones who were winning. Now, U.S. sports psychologists are teaching our athletes to think along similar lines."

–Thomas Sterner

I'll end this article with a deep truth I believe for everyone:

Somehow, you will be taken care of.

Always.

In some mysterious way, everything will turn out beautifully for you.

Therefore, do not be afraid of whether you reach your goals.

Focus instead on your systems.

Use those systems everyday to grow yourself.

Then, the journey of life becomes purposeful and more joyful.

And you may even travel well beyond your original goals.

To watch the companion video or comment on this chapter, go here: www.bit.ly/jpv2c2

3. Go with the Flow vs. Scheduled Flow

To be creative, should you "go with the flow" or schedule out your day?

Consider your relationship to deadlines.

Some people work well by giving themselves due dates. Others avoid it and prefer to "go with the flow."

Either way can work... as long as we make the choice consciously, and thereby be accepting of the results that occur (or don't occur).

If we "go with the flow," we need to accept that we probably won't reach our time-based goals... or that goals may constantly change based on our whims or other people's requests.

On the other hand, if you want to set a vision, have goals, and achieve them within a timeline, then you need to have a good relationship with deadlines, especially the ones you set for yourself.

Call them due dates, milestones, or lifelines, or any other word that energizes you.

Consider the following 3 ways of being.

1. Go with the flow.

This can work well if you are already financially secure, or if you don't need to achieve results within specific timelines. You can accept whatever comes with your lifestyle.

This may also mean accepting the resulting lack of material growth. Don't set goals that are likely to disappoint. Learn to want what you're given. Flow with whatever comes.

Total acceptance is a deep spiritual practice.

The person I most respect for deeply committing to this lifestyle is Peace Pilgrim. She embraced it from a place of deep service to humanity and spiritual growth. She was homeless and simply served everyone. She walked until given food or shelter, helping people wherever she went. She was deeply happy and many people consider her to be very spiritually realized. I highly recommend listening to her audiobook, which is free online: Peace Pilgrim Audiobook.

Unfortunately, that's not how most people "go with the flow." They give into their unwise habits and serve baser appetites, and then they wonder why they aren't able to fulfill the goals they set.

In other words, they actually go with an *unconscious, untrained* flow.

A reader wrote to me:

"Last year, I had the time and money to do everything I wanted. So I went with the flow. But my 'flow' was 'I don't feel good, I'm gonna watch TV or do music'. But I felt empty. I had everything I wanted, but I felt useless and alone. Going with the flow is good for certain things like visiting a city and letting yourself discover the streets... Going with the flow is good when you don't have any goal, want, need in a given situation, or more precisely when your goal is *not* to have a goal. But we all need structure to some point, or we're at the risk of falling into depression."

Let's look at the complete opposite approach.

2. Scheduled Performance.

Many successful people work in this way (although it's not the only way to succeed).

Think of Michael Phelps, the most decorated Olympian of all time. When he was training and competing, just about every minute was scheduled, whether it was swim practice, or rest, or meals. Everything was strictly regimented so that he could optimize his time and life energy for the highest athletic performance.

The same goes with some high-powered executives and celebrities: they often have their work day scheduled down to the 5-minute mark.

In this mode, you schedule everything and expect yourself to show up fully optimized for that activity. You've set high stakes for every hour of the workday.

This is a very challenging way to live, and probably not something most of us aim for.

Let's explore a middle way.

3. Scheduled Flow.

This is what I aim for.

During my work day, I live by a schedule set in 30-minute segments.

I look at my calendar frequently, and do whatever the calendar (my faithful assistant!) says to do.

This method brings out the best of "go with the *flow*" and *"scheduled* performance." Whatever task I've scheduled myself to do, I embrace by going with the flow *within that task.* I aim to enjoy the task itself, without forcing myself to "perform" or achieve an "optimal" result.

In other words, I make sure I show up for the task I've scheduled (left-brained), and then I allow my creativity and intuition to guide me within that task (right-brained.)

I'm not always perfect at using this method, but Scheduled Flow is a practice I keep coming back to, again and again. I do the work for its own sake and aim to apply mindfulness and joyfulness within the work, no matter how the results turn out.

This is how I'm writing this chapter now. I have a deadline that I need to write and post this by 12pm. Am I nervous, anxious, and hustling? No. I've practiced just letting my fingers flow. Whatever words come out (based on a theme I pre-set) — and I edit lightly — is what you'll end up reading.

(This chapter started as a more casual blog post, and has since gone through the careful editing of several of my wonderful supporters – thank you Brigitte and Faith!)

What about the results?

Based on years of experimenting with this method, I now know that if I show up consistently to practice joyful productivity in the moment, and let go of pressuring myself to achieve results, I tend to accomplish a lot over time. In addition, rather than feeling anxious, I feel more graceful and calm during the process.

I've long been inspired by this passage from the Bhagavad Gita:

"To action alone has thou a right, and never at all to its fruits;
Let not the fruits of action be thy motive;
Neither let there be in thou any attachment to inaction. . . .
Therefore, without being attached to the fruits of activities, one
should act as a matter of duty,
For by working without attachment one attains the Supreme."

Stay with the Process

The key to making this work is to stay with the task that I've scheduled even if I don't feel like it. I don't allow myself to get distracted and "go with the flow" and pursue other tasks.

I stay with what I planned to do. If it turns out that it was not a great plan, then I've learned a lesson to plan better the next time!

Within the task, I'm not afraid of making mistakes because I don't have a set performance result that I "must" achieve.

Of course, just like anyone else, I enjoy wonderful results but I don't require it in the moment. I trust that over time, as I continue to show up for the work, I will naturally grow the skills and confidence to get better results, without having to try too hard.

Whether the results are "good" or not, the better question I ask myself is whether the *process* was good. Was I mindful? Did I enjoy the work? Was it compassionate and aligned with my values?

If you're going to avoid deadlines and due dates, and want to go with the flow, then be accepting that Life will give you whatever It wants to... You may find yourself confronted with demanding tasks you don't feel like doing but end up "having to" do.

Instead, can we create a new and healthier relationship to deadlines?

Let's practice setting goals and deadlines (or lifelines) as our compass and journey joyfully.

Let's work towards our goals with playful experimentation and curiosity, appreciating the learning and the moment-by-moment process.

To watch the companion video or comment on this chapter, go here: www.bit.ly/jpv2c3

4. True Productivity for Self-Employed Professionals

What are the most productive actions in your business?

Checking off more items on your to-do list? Working longer hours? Getting another certification? Trying to make your website better?

Many such actions feel productive but don't actually build your business. Besides having a "to do" list, you may want to define a "to-drop" list as well.

Otherwise you might be doing busy work that feels like movement but isn't really helping you grow your client base or boost your impact.

Here is how I define "true productivity" in business:

Valuable interaction with the people your business can best serve.

It means being in touch with your market, rather than being in your own head.

You'll know that it's a valuable interaction, and an ideal audience, if it inspires reciprocity of some kind (likes, comments, shares, inquiries, purchases). If an activity doesn't inspire reciprocity (in the short term) from your audience, you should question that activity and modify it until it does.

Who is your ideal audience? Who are the people your business can best serve?

- Clients (current, prospective, and former)

- Referral sources (current and prospective)

- True fans (those who regularly engage or share your content)

Be suspicious of any work activity that doesn't include being in contact with one of these groups.

My Truly Productive TO-DO List

Here are some examples from my own to-do list:

- Creating and publishing content for my ideal audience (not spending too much time perfecting it)
- Paid advertising to increase the reach of my content (Facebook Ads, Instagram Ads, Google Ads)
- Engaging on the meaningful comments left on my posts
- Contacting fans or colleagues about doing a market research conversation
- Getting feedback from my audience about my offering (e.g. the draft of a sales page.)
- Announcing my next offering (course or program) via email newsletter and social media
- Paid advertising to make sure my warm audience sees the upcoming offering a few times
- Reaching out to prospective clients to offer an ex-

ploratory call or sample session (Update: since 2018 I've stopped doing this, as I have a waiting list — thanks to the other actions on this list!)

- Contacting current clients to schedule the next session(s) if needed

- Getting feedback from my clients about how to improve my services

- Reaching out to referral partners to schedule a mutual support networking call or collaboration

- Preparing for a client meeting or upcoming course (not perfection... just enough prep)

- Being truly present in meetings with clients, students, and colleagues

- Sending an email newsletter to my subscribers with my latest content

- Writing a book / course, on a schedule, so that I publish rather than perfect

- Implementing a course or article that helps me do one of the above

- Asking a question on social media or in a group, that will help me get unstuck on doing one of the above

- Getting 1–1 coaching/consulting to help me do one of the above

- Eliminating or delegating as much of everything else as possible

- Interspersing various forms of self-care as needed throughout my work day, e.g. naps, walks, meals, energy reboot, etc.

The above 20 actions are what I spend my working days on.

This is how I stay truly productive.

Questionable TO-DROP List

The following are the tempting items that seem productive but need to be continually questioned if it's happening during working hours.

- Doing small tweaks to try to perfect your website even more. (I only make changes to my website to correct errors on commonly-visited pages or to add in new content that I'm certain I want to keep on my website for at least 3 months.)

- Working on a future event, program, service, course, or book — **if it isn't already announced** — versus announcing it, therefore giving a deadline to work on it more efficiently.

- Reading articles and books, unless you are *implementing* as you read (otherwise I do it in my free time).

- Watching videos, unless you are implementing as you watch (otherwise I do it in my free time).

- Listening to podcasts. (I do this in my free time, not working hours.)

- Doing research for a blog post, video, or even a paid course, unless there's a clear time limit and the audience is expecting it.

- Getting training, unless you also have time scheduled to implement that training.

- Getting another certification because it "might" help your marketing or might help you feel more credible.

- Updating your social media profile "about" sections. (I do this *at most* once a year.)

- Reading or commenting in groups, unless I'm actively getting help. (After posting my question, I try to be a good group citizen and comment on two other threads to help out, but I don't just "hang out" in the group.)

- Researching on the Internet, Google searches, on anything for more than 5 minutes, unless I'm implementing in the moment. Otherwise, I do exploratory research in my free time.

- Any kind of planning, plotting, preparing, unless it is directly related to a Truly Productive action that is scheduled and, ideally, announced to my audience so that I have a true deadline rather than *the danger of eternal preparation.*

In summary, I minimize the work that I do in isolation. Whenever possible, I am always getting feedback from the market or being in valuable contact with my ideal audience via content, offerings, or conversations.

I encourage you to write down your own lists:

Truly Productive TO-DO List

Questionable TO-DROP List

Of course, you're welcome to borrow from my lists above!

I wish you joyful – and true – productivity.

To watch the companion video or comment on this chapter, go here: www.bit.ly/trulyproductivevideo

5. Define Your Daily Success

The most common financial goal for solopreneurs?
To make "6 figures."

(And if they achieve that, they now have to make "7 figures" because you can never make enough, right?)

How do you relate to goals?

Do you set ones that are effective — and mentally healthy — for you?

While there is some science indicating that having "big hairy audacious goals" can inspire and motivate *organizations* of people, I wonder if it actually helps you, as a self-employed person, take **consistent** action. Do the BHAGs help you work on strategic tasks with joyful productivity every day?

Many of us have felt discouraged or disillusioned due to a past fixation on big goals that didn't work out.

Here's the thing: you weren't born with the goal of "making 6 figures." Someone else gave you that definition of success. With all of their marketing to you, you started to believe that it's your goal, too.

Maybe it's inspiring to consume motivational content about huge goals, 7 figures, going to the moon, etc. But does it actually help you to take strategic action every day?

If you frequently look at your income and you're not yet at "6 figures," it's natural to feel like it's so far off. Self-blame might even creep in.

By selling you that dream, business gurus can then sell you on expensive programs, because you'll be earning 6 figures anyway, so their program price now seems like a drop in the bucket!

Just like them, having that singular focus on high income can get you to compromise your values and your heart. You're told that you need to do "whatever it takes," which often includes marketing tactics that don't feel aligned with you... the same tactics used on you by those business gurus.

If those high goals are bringing you discouragement and mis-alignment, then you need to consciously detach from that brainwashing. Unsubscribe from their newsletters. Stop follow-ing them on social media. Otherwise, you'll just keep getting influenced.

Instead, define your own version of "success". Remind yourself of it every day.

Instead of "6 figures," set a more doable goal for the next 3 months: "Increase my income from $0 to $300 per month... or $1,000 to $1,500 per month... or $3,000 to $4,000 per month..."

Make a goal that feels *truly doable* for you within a *short* time frame.

By having a realistic goal at the forefront of your consciousness, you will tap your creativity in a more productive way, because you will "see" and feel the possibility of achieving that goal.

You will really believe (without affirmations) that it's doable for you.

It's the difference between "you still have a marathon to run!" and "let's run the next mile... with joy!"

You might even find yourself surpassing your goal sooner than you thought! This has consistently happened to me year after year. I set realistic goals, and focus daily on joyful productivity... and am continually delighted that I reach and surpass those goals.

As you focus daily on what is doable today or this month, you'll find yourself achieving doable goals consistently, which means you'll be building your **confidence**, too.

You'll get to **celebrate** a lot more along the way! Instead of saying that you're successful when you get to "6 figures," you can now enjoy the whole journey. By focusing on each realistic milestone, you'll experience success more often.

Before you know it, you may actually reach (and surpass) 6 figures. But let's not focus daily on that huge goal... until one day, you discover that you're actually quite close to it!

So the next time a biz expert flaunts their 6- or 7-figure income and says "you can do this too!" maybe you should just unsubscribe.

Set doable goals, stretch just a little bit each day, and always come back to your own joyful productivity.

To watch the companion video or comment on this chapter, go here: www.bit.ly/jpv2c5

6. The EADA Productivity Method

Not everything on your to-do list is meant to be done by you.

As you look at each task, does it fit all 3 criteria?

1. **Enjoyment**: You do (or wish to) enjoy doing it.

2. **Expertise**: You are (or wish to become) an expert at it.

3. **Effect**: This task has more worthwhile effects compared to other tasks you could do now.

If it passes all 3 checks, then the task is worth your action, with mindfulness and deliberate practice.

If it doesn't pass all 3 checks, then you need to consider one of these 4 actions. . .

Eliminate
Automate
Delegate
Appreciate

I'll explain each.

Eliminate

The fact that you are reading about productivity means that you're more conscientious than most people. You tend to carry a lot on your shoulders.

You have far more items on your to-do list than you have time for.

For your mental health — and the opportunity to shift your time to what's truly worthwhile — it is time to practice eliminating tasks from your list.

Maybe you fear erasing the task from your to-do list, wondering *"what if I need this later?"*

That question is what leads to clutter and overwhelm.

Instead, practice just getting rid of it. You're practicing the all-important skill of *simplifying.*

When you feel the fear of missing out or losing out on potential opportunity, take a moment: do whatever it is that helps you to reconnect with your limitless source of abundance within.

You might observe that you actually need to do relatively little to be fine.

If you are still hesitating to delete a task, quickly run it through the three criteria above: Enjoyment? Expertise? Effect? It must be a strong "Yes," for all three, to stay on your list.

As an option, you can remove the due date and transfer the task to a "someday / maybe" pile so that it doesn't keep bugging you.

If you see a task appear again and again — and it doesn't meet the Enjoy, Expert, Effect criteria — then it's time to either Automate or Delegate it.

Automate

Machines and software are getting increasingly more capable. Almost all of our "work" will become automated eventually. Studies are showing that huge swaths of human industry will be taken over by robotics and artificial intelligence.

Resistance is futile...

...and unnecessary!

If you believe that the purpose of life has something to do with growing in love and wisdom, then we humans are being called to ever higher levels of work: to bring more creativity, caring, connectedness into our work than machines can.

It's time to stop doing tasks that don't meet your Enjoy, Expert, Effect criteria. If the task keeps coming up, find a way to automate it.

A few examples:

- Instead of back and forth emails for scheduling, I use AcuityScheduling.

- Instead of manual data entry, I use Zapier.

- Instead of manually moving newsletters into "read later," I use gmail's filters.

Delegate

If there's no available technology to automate your recurring tasks that don't pass your Enjoy/Expert/Effect filter, it's time to hire someone to do it for you, if you have the budget.

To vet your own assistants and freelancers, there are two websites I recommend getting familiar with:

www.Fiverr.com — Hire a freelancer to do your graphic design, website creation / management, Internet research, copywriting/editing, audio or video editing, spreadsheet improvement, transcription, all kinds of technological troubleshooting, and many other virtual tasks. For example, I used Fiverr to get book cover designs, convert my book to Kindle version and format it for paperback publishing, and edit/master my audiobook.

www.Upwork.com — A searchable directory of millions of freelancers that can do all kinds of things for your business. A couple of examples of my successful hires: researching best places to live in Mexico; tax prep and filing that is affordable, accurate, and fast.

The sky's the limit as to what you can find on Fiverr and Upwork.

What about the low fees? Is it unethical? I'll let you decide:

A software engineer in the Philippines, or Pakistan, both earn about $6 to $8 USD per hour.

If you could pay them $10/hour, allowing them to work as a freelancer, it's a better lifestyle for them. Your money makes a much bigger difference in their life, compared to paying someone in a first world country.

A couple of helpful notes about outsourcing:

1. Some of the people you hire will want to do more work for you than your business actually needs. If you hire them by the hour, they are incentivized in that way. Be smart and only outsource the tasks that are truly productive. You may want to check in with a business-savvy colleague or a coach before you spend money outsourcing a task or project.

2. Once you've determined tasks that are truly productive to outsource, then *hire quickly*. Don't get bogged down trying to pick the perfect person. It's almost impossible to know in advance, unless they have consistently bad reviews. I've worked with some of the best freelancers who had no reviews, so don't be afraid to give someone new a try. Hire quickly, but here's the next key:

3. Give a small task first, and if they do well, a slightly bigger task, and then increase your trust in them in that way.

4. If at any point (including the small task) there's a doubt in your mind they're the right person, it's best to *quickly* end the contract/project with them as appropriate, and go onto trying the next freelancer. This is why you should try out a small task with them first.

5. Often, for an important project, I will hire several free-lancers to do the same small task, to see which one I'll give the next bigger task to.

Appreciate

Another way to filter out things you really shouldn't be doing is to ask:

"What tasks am I resentful about?"

Make a list of such tasks.

Eliminate them.

If you must keep the task, can you Automate it?
If you can't, then can you Delegate it?
If you can't, then the only thing left is to Appreciate it.

Do your inner work, or work with a coach, to make that task something you can truly enjoy. I believe that any task can be made enjoyable if we are willing to open up to that possibility.

The world will be a better place if we can each spend our energy doing the things we *enjoy*, want to be *expert* at, and are truly *effective* uses of our time.

To watch the companion video or comment on this chapter, go here: www.bit.ly/jpv2c6

7. The Energy Reboot

This is a simple spiritual practice that I do multiple times a day that has made a profound and positive difference in my work.

Since it takes only 30 seconds, I do it at least three times each working hour (except when in a meeting). In other words, I meditate for about nine minutes per day... it's just split up into about 18 thirty-second meditations throughout the day. I find it so helpful.

I call it the Energy Reboot. Several years ago I published a blog post and video about it: Energy Reboot 1. (If you haven't tried the first version, it's a good starting point.)

Since 2021, I've been using a new version, which I'll describe below. It's a good follow-on for those who have already done Energy Reboot 1 and wish to try something new.

Similar to the previous exercise, this new version also centers around deep breaths, while holding a specific thought per breath.

Each breath in a gentle deep inhale, a gentle slow exhale, a hand/arm movement, all while holding a specific thought...

(I use the word "God" but feel free to replace it with any word that inspires you.)

Breath 1 – both hands on the heart.
"Thank You God for bringing me here to this moment, through all the ups and downs."
(I take a moment to feel deep gratitude.)

Breath 2 – both hands on the lower stomach.
"I know that You'll bring me through everything... through all the ups and downs... all the way Home. Thank You."

Breath 3 – hands down to each side of the body, palms open and forward, in receiving posture.
"Thank You for the healing, dear Support Team!"
(I try to feel, in my body, that healing energy is moving through me, from my spiritual support team. I often get a momentary shiver or goosebumps, which helps me imagine that it's working.)

Breath 4 – taking a nice big stretch, hands all the way above my head.
"Thank You for this moment of practice."
(A moment of commitment to the practice of joyful productivity.)

Breath 5 – hands slowly back down, ready to work.
"Thank You for giving me everything I need for this moment of work. May I bring Love."

I do this at the start of each work hour – and several more times during the hour, especially when I notice I feel stuck on a project. No matter what, I aim to do this Energy Reboot about once every 20-30 minutes during my working day. Sometimes, as often as every 5-10 minutes, if it's a tough task.

An important point: this practice takes only 30 seconds. Keeping it short makes it more likely that I'll do it often.

Doing it **often** is key to shifting our state of being. It creates joyful productivity on a consistent basis.

No matter how much of a hurry I'm in, I know that I can take 30 seconds to bring in good energy. If we are committed to living and working in a higher-quality way, we can't afford *not* to infuse our next moment with good energy.

At the end of a work period, I'll do this practice again to reset myself for the next hour and to give thanks for having been brought through. *"I knew that you would bring me through this hour. Yet again. Thank You."*

It also helps that these breaths are tied to hand and arm movements. It makes the affirmed thought (of gratitude or faith) more embodied, more integrated into my body's core feelings and way of being.

This 30 second practice seems subtle, but when done frequently, it allows me to move through every day with greater grace and productivity, no matter how distracting or tough the day is.

I hope you'll give it a try and see if it helps you. Again, the key is to do it frequently, not just once or twice a day.

To watch the companion video or comment on this chapter, go here: www.bit.ly/jpv2c7

8. Be Strict about Showing Up, Lenient about the Results

A client asked: "George, how do you stay with such a regimented schedule... yet remain calm and joyful as you work?"

Every workday, I stick to a schedule, getting a lot done in an easeful manner, without undue strain. And yet, even with a full day of appointments and projects, I don't feel like I'm in a hurry when I meet with clients. I can still be my creative self with them.

It has taken a lot of practice. Here's the key:

I'm strict about showing up, lenient about results... and gentle to bring myself back to focus, again and again.

This is the core mode of operation I've had for years. It brings a deep sense of self-empowerment, showing me that I can accomplish anything I intend to, as long as I'm willing to show up consistently, time after time.

Sadly, many do the opposite.

People who are heart-centered givers (including some who are reading this right now) tend to be **lenient** about showing up on time for their own work, yet so **strict** with themselves about the results. They tend to spiral into perfectionism, self-doubt, and harsh self-criticism. When they realize they've gotten distracted, they tend to self-blame.

If that describes you, it's no wonder that you procrastinate — you're reluctant to show up because you're afraid of self-punishment!

There's no blame here. Almost none of us were raised with a philosophy of joyful productivity. I certainly wasn't.

Once we realize the power of this method, we can commit to it and truly change ourselves.

It takes continuous mindfulness and reframing to come to the understanding that you only need to be strict about showing up, yet lenient with results, and gentle about re-focusing.

Here's an example of this philosophy in action:
https://youtu.be/HAlyE29ybzI

I didn't feel like making the above video. I was visiting my parents for the weekend. I wasn't in a place where I was comfortable making videos, and wondered what people in the park would think. I wasn't feeling inspired.

But I showed up anyway.

I just started recording, and allowed myself to speak about the main points I'd planned. (A few days earlier, I had been "strict" about showing up to outline my content.)

I didn't worry about the result of the video. I did a few takes, but that's normal for pre-recorded videos. It took me 15 minutes to make this 5-minute video.

This is an example of being strict with my time but lenient as to what happens during that time... as long as I'm doing what

I planned. If I get distracted temporarily, I gently bring myself back to the task.

Just like in meditation or prayer, when your mind wanders, there's no need for self-blame. Just gently bring your mind back to your meditation or prayer.

The key? No matter how I'm feeling, I show up anyway to do what I had planned.

I never feel like it...

Here's a secret:I never feel like making my weekly videos.

Also, I never feel like writing my blog posts.

Why not? It's because of creative discomfort: the potential anxiety or fear of not knowing what to say, or of saying the wrong things, or of being judged by others (and by myself).

But I've learned that if I show up anyway, I eventually find a flow after the initial discomfort. I just need to be strict about showing up, starting the work, and seeing what happens with continued action and gentle wrestling.

Skill and results naturally grow over time, when we keep showing up, day after day.

Don't force yourself to have "good results" during any one work period. Look at "results" from a long-term perspective: the process of gradual improvement.

Just show up for the work. Stay on task, gently bringing yourself back again and again to focus, almost as a spiritual practice.

I'm lenient with my results in that I don't worry about the quality of what is produced during that hour, as long as I'm doing the work I planned. It might end up being a crappy video, or a poorly-written article, or maybe I'm studying some complex topic, and I still don't understand it after an hour.

I practice avoiding self-judgment. (Yes, it's a practice until it becomes natural.) What matters is that I keep producing. With consistent practice, I know that skills will naturally increase, and my results will inevitably improve over time.

Becoming free of self-judgment

How to become free of your own self-judgment? I'm going to guess that you already have a tool or modality that has worked for you in the past. Now you simply need to practice it regularly. Use any method that works for you.

What works for me? The Energy Reboot.

At the beginning of any work period, I use the energy reboot practice to gently remind myself of what I believe to be true about Life: that we are all eternally secure in an inevitable path towards complete Goodness. We are lovingly taken care of, in deeper and grander ways than we can imagine.

No, I don't have a trust fund, but I feel secure because we all have an inner spiritual resource that is inexhaustible. I'm grateful that I can tap into it anytime.

I believe that it's our higher work to practice tapping into that inner resource on a daily basis, so that we can work in a state of gentle focus. We practice being reliable and showing up on time, not only for others but for ourselves, too.

Taking breaks

Besides showing up for work reliably, I'm also strict about taking breaks, even when I don't feel like it.

Again, this is opposite of what many people do: they only take a break after they've exhausted themselves.

If we take breaks and renew ourselves before we get tired, we will tend to enjoy our work more and experience more creativity.

On a regular basis (every 25–50 minutes) get up! Move around. You'll find new ideas coming to you with less mental effort.

(A tool that has helped me to practice showing up on time, as well as taking breaks, is Focusmate. I usually have 3-5 Focusmate sessions every workday.)

If you haven't been producing as much work as you'd like to, or if you're not working joyfully, I recommend that you give this philosophy a try.

Be strict about showing up on time for your own work, no matter what.

Be lenient (not self-judging) about the results of your work, knowing that it'll get better over time.

Be "gently strict" about the whole process, continuing to bring your attention back to the planned work, again and again.

I hope you will also try out this philosophy, and let me know how it goes for you!

To watch the companion video or comment on this chapter, go here: www.bit.ly/jpv2c8

9. Conscious Systems Design for a Better Life & Business

Your life is actually working perfectly.

And your business? It's exactly where it's supposed to be.

It's not that you love all the results.

However, anything and everything occurring in your life *has a system behind it.* There's cause and effect. You experience the **effects...** and you have more choice in the **causes** than you realize.

It's true that there are some causes beyond your control, but you always have a choice of **where you focus.**

You can blame others for the bad effects in life — other people, the economy, your upbringing, genetics, karma, or the stars — but every time you do this, you give some of your power away.

I invite you to take on this idea:

"I am more in control of my life experience than I can imagine."

In other words, it is possible to engage with *conscious* systems design.

I believe that many of the results I'm getting are due to the systems I have allowed or created in my life.

Therefore, I actively redesign the systems, leading me to different results.

Let's explore a few examples of situations that are within our control.

If you are always **waking up late**, the system might go like this...

1. You cannot wake up and feel refreshed unless you get enough sleep.
2. Because you go to sleep *late*, you have to wake up *late*.
3. You sleep late because you *start* your evening routine late.

Once you diagnose a cause you can control, you can design a new system:

- You can plan a new evening routine that allows you to go to sleep earlier.
- You can set a reminder to **start** your evening routine earlier.

Even something as simple as **going to bed on time** is a system that impacts many other systems in your life. The better you sleep, the more optimistic you feel, and the more you feel empowered to take action in other areas.

"Time management is really the management of routines....The purpose of routines is not to turn you into some sort of automa-

ton, but to free your consciousness to work at a higher level." — *Mark Forster*

Another example:

If your alarms/reminders aren't helping you, here's the system...

1. The reminder/alarm goes off.
2. You ignore it, and continue doing what you were doing.
3. Therefore, you cannot follow a schedule that is healthy for you.

This system can be changed. I wrote about it here: Deliberate Practice and Joyful Productivity

Another example:

You wish for less time at the computer.

The system behind it is that you get mesmerized or "stuck" at the computer for hours without taking a break.

I wrote about a better system called Rest Before Your Need To.

Another example:

Your email inbox is continually giving you stress.

The system behind how you process email is broken. I've written about a better email processing routine.

Final example:

You have projects you aren't getting done. You keep procrastinating.

Your system for how you think about that project needs to change. I call it your <u>motivational methods</u>.

What's not working well in your life or business?

Write about a possible system that you can tweak so that you may create different results.

Sometimes you will need to research how to modify a system. Look for routines, plans, processes, templates, checklists, structures, or habits that people like you are using to get better results.

Other times you may want to work with a coach or therapist who specializes in that issue. The best ones help you design a system for your specific situation, then help you form solid habits of applying the better system.

It also helps if you study what **is** working well in your life. Which of your systems generate good results? This helps you better understand yourself and what systems are compatible for you.

In other words, the systems that you ***allow*** to continue in your life are working ***just the way*** they're supposed to. If the results are good, it's a good system for you. If the results are "bad," you need to re-design the system.

As you become increasingly conscious of your life's systems, you'll have more choice about changing them.

Step by step, you can transform any system in your life. You can gradually create a life that you absolutely love!

To watch the companion video or comment on this chapter, go here: www.bit.ly/jpv2c9

10. How to Effectively Use Visualization to Achieve Goals

Visualize the process, not just the outcome

Millions of people have tried the "Law Of Attraction" (popularized by "The Secret") ... and no matter how hard they try, they don't manifest those millions of dollars they envisioned.

If they go into debt to buy that fancy house or car, they usually regret the debt. Or that so-called "perfect" relationship they visualized doesn't end up working out.

Visualization is ineffective – even detrimental – when used **only** to imagine the ideal outcome.

Instead, what if we use visualization to strengthen *the process of our actions* towards the desired outcome?

If we can manifest a joyful way of working day to day, rather than pining for a better future, we give ourselves the best chance at creating our ideal life.

There are 2 things that make this work:

1. Successful visualization focuses on the process, even more than the outcome.

2. Visualization is a fantasy, unless tied closely to real-world practice.

Focusing on the Process

Most people visualize only the desired outcomes.

"I've written my best-selling book... I'm holding it in my hands... I'm seeing hundreds of positive reviews!"

"I've filled my workshop... I see a large group of students who are joyfully experiencing transformation!"

"I've filled my practice with ideal clients... I imagine myself working with high-paying clients on a typical workday!"

These are good mental pictures to have, insofar as they:

- Help you feel that the end vision is possible to attain
- Help you see what *direction* to work towards

It can, however, be detrimental to *merely* create the self-belief that you "deserve" it.

Your vision may be ungrounded from the reality of what it actually takes to achieve it. You might also develop a false belief that you are **entitled** to it... and when you don't attain that vision which you frequently repeat, it creates even more self-doubt than when you started.

By failing to achieve your dream, you might even doubt the tool of visualization!

Let's take a deep breath.

There's a better way to use visualization.

Here is what we all truly "deserve" – **to improve our journey/process.**

A good process eventually leads to a good outcome.

Consistent actions, in the right direction, create miraculous results over time!

In the book *The Compound Effect* by Darren Hardy, he tells the story of two people:

- Aaron takes a job for $5,000/month, a job that uses only his existing skills.
- Barbara starts a business that earns her $10 in the first week, but with repeated improvement in her skills, it results in 10% growth in income each week.

Observe the wealth of these two people:

- 3rd month: total of $15,000 (Aaron) versus $235 (Barbara)
- 12th month: total of $60,000 versus $15,000
- 18th month: total of $90,000 versus $186,000
- 24th month: total of $120,000 (Aaron) versus $2.2 million (Barbara)

Again, consistent actions, with consistent small improvements, create the kind of results that many only visualize, but never manifest. Therefore, visualize *enjoying the process* so that you'll do it consistently, growing gradually in your skill and joy!

I'm grateful that my books have received many good reviews, but I didn't use outcome-visualization, except to help me believe that it was possible, and to make plans. Then, I used process-visualization every day to enjoy the tasks needed to accomplish those grand plans.

So instead of seeing yourself with a best-selling book, visualize the circumstances in which you are writing your book:

- What day and time are you writing?
- Where are you?
- What did you do before you started writing, and how did you get into it? (This helps to anchor the task in reality.)
- What tool are you using to write, and how are you using it?
- What's the expression on your face as you write?
- What joyful feelings are coming up, as you write?
- What else about your body and action can you visualize? For example, are you taking gentle, easy deep breaths as you write?

Another example: instead of seeing yourself with a full roster of clients, how about seeing yourself <u>sending thoughtful emails to your prospective clients and referral sources</u> and doing it from a feeling of connection, joy, and service?

If you focus on the process, you are more likely to attain the outcome.

This is what visualization can really help with: being consistent with the process, and along the way, enjoying your actions!

Learning Visualization through Practice

Many people don't connect their visualization to what they *actually* do day to day, hour by hour. Too often, they do visualization as a separate activity in the morning or evening, reading out loud their dreams and "seeing" in their mind's eye what they want.

Instead, I encourage you to visualize the process (for example, the action of writing the book) and then when the time comes to do the action, observe yourself as you actually write the book, and ask:

"What don't I **love** about this process? How can I visualize an even more joyful process?"

It's this ongoing dialogue with yourself that makes visualization truly effective:

Step 1. Visualize the desired outcome so that you believe you can do it.

Step 2. Visualize the process (the actions you'll actually take toward your desired outcome).

Step 3. Do the process that you visualized, while noticing what you're not enjoying.

(If you observe the process, then you can improve it!)

Step 4. Visualize an *improved* process.

Step 5. Practice the improved process as soon as possible.

Keep repeating these steps every day, so that you enjoy your journey more and more. You will make real progress on your biggest goals!

Process-visualization starts creating a bit of muscle memory. The practice of the actions strengthens that muscle memory. Your mindfulness about the process allows you to see what you need to adjust, so that you can enjoy the actions even more.

Eventually, you'll get to an advanced state where you don't even need to set aside time to visualize anymore. You'll find yourself being able to easily imagine what outcome you want, and then take actions from a practiced state of joyful productivity.

To watch the companion video or comment on this chapter, go here: www.bit.ly/jpv2c10

11. Sleep Tips—Falling and Staying Asleep

Building a thriving, authentic business requires you to cultivate multiple habits. If I had to name *one habit* that I would encourage everyone to start with, it would be to practice better sleep.

Surprising? Maybe not, if you understand that better sleep is required to have the energy to plan strategically, to be creative, to set boundaries, and everything else that's part of effectively managing your time and relationships.

Allow me to share with you what works for me to sleep better. I also welcome your comments on what works for you.

One-Time Preparations

Get blackout curtains for your bedroom. Even a sliver of light can affect your sleep, so try to make your bedroom as dark as possible each night.

If light is coming from outside your bedroom door, get a door draft stopper.

Irregular sounds can randomly wake you, so try to soundproof your bedroom. (The blackout curtains and draft stopper will help.) You might also get a <u>white noise machine</u>, which is inexpensive and can help to block out sounds and maintain a steady audio environment for you to sleep. The cheapest way, of course, is to use ear plugs, especially if you sleep with a snoring partner.

If you're sometimes too hot or cold, you might need a bed pad to keep the temperature steady enough for you to sleep through the night. I bought a <u>chiliPAD Cube</u> a few years ago, and I still use it every night.

Nightly Preparations

As day turns to night, your willpower tends to decrease because you've been using it all day. Ironically, we need energy (willpower) to get ourselves to bed. Make it easier for yourself by having a clear, unambiguous step-by-step plan for how you wind down and go to bed.

For example:

- set an alarm to indicate it's time to get up from the TV or laptop
- wash the dishes (how long does it take?)
- feed the animals (how long?)
- use the bathroom (how long?)
- do your evening hygiene (how long?)
- ... so that you can finally get into bed.

Write out a specific plan for how many minutes each of these tasks takes you. Then set an alarm for exactly when you'll start the process each night, so that by the time you get into bed, you still get enough sleep.

It also helps me to stop drinking any liquid within three hours of bedtime. I was quite uncomfortable with this, but I started practicing bit by bit... stopping liquids 30 minutes before bed, then eventually one hour, and gradually stopping up to three hours. Now, I'm quite used to it. Any change is possible if you take time to slowly habituate into it!

Moving My Sleep Time

I used to be a night owl, getting to bed at about midnight, and still it was a struggle to fall asleep.

Now, I easily sleep at 10:30 pm. How? It required a gradual change over many weeks.

Our bodies have a delicate equilibrium; the body clock wants consistency, with any changes being as gradual as possible.

I slowly moved my bedtime from midnight to 10:30 pm. I set a daily alarm to begin my evening hygiene routine. Every few nights, I shifted that alarm time five minutes earlier, until many weeks later, I was able to be in bed, lights out, by 10:30.

The SPA Method

Once you're in bed, lights out, how do you fall and stay asleep? I used to have so many thoughts before bed, often waking up in the middle of the night with a strong desire to write or plan things. I learned that it just made my next day feel terrible because I didn't get enough rest.

Now, I use the following method to fall asleep, and if I awake in the middle of the night, I use this same method to fall back asleep. I use this method as many times as needed.

The steps spell SPA, and it's also nice because we can imagine ourselves being in a relaxing spa environment.

S = Sixty seconds to stillness

Once I'm in bed and lights out, I start counting up from 0, and try to adjust my position and the blanket and the pillow and everything else, before I get to the count of 60, to feel comfortable enough to move to the next step.

The key to falling asleep is to stop moving! **Stop moving** your body and slow down your mind.

This is why I give myself those 60 seconds to move just enough to find that *good-enough* position. I think "as long as I'm not in pain, I can *stop moving* long enough until I feel sleepy... then adjust a little more if I need to at that point."

P = Peaceful healing breath

Once I'm still, I start to think "peaceful healing breath."

Peace on the in-breath.

Healing on the out-breath.

I try to imagine myself experiencing peaceful healing. This gets a little weird, but stay with me...

There's a near-death experience by a veteran named Natalie Sudman where she talked about entering the "healing environment" in the spirit world, where her spirit helpers were repairing her body. She ended up with a miraculous physical recovery.

I imagine that I am entering such a healing space and that my spirit helpers are replacing the molecules in my various organs with better molecules.

Whatever way helps you to imagine yourself being healed, use it!

A = Appreciation

Usually, the stillness and peaceful healing breath will have me asleep within 10 minutes.

If I still find myself awake, I move into appreciation.

I start appreciating various things in my life.

I begin with my faith: I believe that I have a spiritual support team with me at all times, including right there supporting me in the bedroom. That often helps me fall asleep.

If still awake, I move into appreciating something physical about this moment. It doesn't have to be perfect. Maybe the pillow is somewhat comfortable tonight. Or maybe the blanket. Whatever one thing I can appreciate, I focus on that, and enjoy the moment.

If I am still awake, I go on to appreciating other aspects of my life.

**

So that's the method that helps me fall asleep. And if I randomly find myself awake in the middle of the night, I use the same SPA method to fall back asleep.

Give it a try and let me know if it helps!

Middle-of-Night Meditation

I've been a very light sleeper all my life. For years I had trouble falling asleep. With the SPA method and all the other preparations mentioned above, I now fall asleep much quicker.

However, still to this day, I find myself awake, frequently, every night.

I simply practice the SPA method again, until I fall asleep.

It's my middle-of-night meditation.

The power of meditation is that it's always there for us. We can just gently guide ourselves back to the meditative process whenever needed. It is a calming and healing energetic space we can create for ourselves. Even if I'm not asleep like I want to, I know that my body and mind are being healed, and that energy is being regenerated, if I continue to gently practice the SPA meditation.

I've learned from experience that I simply need to stay in bed, relaxing, with eyes closed. Don't get up. This is counter to the mainstream advice about insomnia, which tells us to *not* stay in bed awake. But I've noticed if I get up in the middle of the night for even half an hour and go back to sleep afterwards, I feel very tired the next day.

Strangely, as long as I stay in bed for about 8 hours, I feel fine the next day, even if I was awake for a few hours, gently practicing the SPA meditation. Stay in bed, relaxing, eyes closed.

Every Body is Different

However, every person's bodily system is different.

There's evidence to suggest that biphasic sleep helps some people. Research shows that some cultures slept in two shifts at night, so that may be helpful to you as well.

What works for me is to take 3 naps each day, about 20 minutes each.

The key is to experiment with your own sleep and see what works best for you.

I would recommend, however, that you be gradual with any changes, and give any new change at least a few weeks for your body to adjust.

Trust

Finally, trust that you're getting enough sleep.

If you weren't, you'd be sleepy often. (If you're already regularly sleeping 8 to10 hours every night, and still feel sleepy, then it may be some medical issue.)

Every night, even though I'm in bed for 7-8 hours, I am unconscious for only 4-5 hours, and have very light sleep for the rest of the hours.

I used to worry about it a lot. I read books about sleep. I bought sleep technology to monitor myself.

One day, I decided to experiment with something: I just stopped worrying about my sleep. I simply did what I've written above – prepared for good sleep and just did what I could.

My sleep hasn't changed that much, but my quality of life has been so much better ever since I stopped worrying about my sleep.

Each of our bodies is so different. Each of us needs a different quantity and quality of sleep. Generally, humans thrive on about 8 hours per night, so try to get that amount of time relaxing, horizontal in bed, but beyond that, just try to relax about your sleep "issues" and you may find that they're really non-issues.

Try these techniques if you'd like, and let me know if it helps!

If you have your own sleep tips to share, feel free to comment below. It might really help someone else.

To watch the companion video or comment on this chapter, go here: www.bit.ly/jpv2c11

12. The Deliberate Practice of Enjoying Every Activity

The secret to joyful productivity is learning how to find enjoyment in any activity – especially tasks that move your goals forward but aren't naturally "fun" to do – being able to do what is important, no matter what it is, with consistent joy.

This chapter will offer some ways to learn this valuable meta-skill.

Muscle Memory

Let's start with the idea of Muscle Memory.

Most of us can walk and talk at the same time. Yet we're born with neither ability.

With practice, you can learn to type without having to look at each letter on the keyboard.

With practice, you can learn any sport you're interested in, even though it requires the coordination of dozens of muscles at a moment's notice.

These are all examples of muscle memory.

Through intentional repetition, any behavior or habit can become instinctual for you.

A closer look at a personal example:

I wanted to solidify my habit of doing the <u>Energy Reboot Practice</u> whenever I start work at the computer. Otherwise, I can easily just plop down in front of the laptop and start doing email or other less intentional activities. Whatever comes instinctually – based on past patterns – isn't always purposeful or optimal.

So I used this idea of muscle memory to break that pattern. I practiced this: I left the room, then came back in (where the computer is), sat down, and did my 30-second energy reboot practice, and then got started on a purposeful task for 1 minute.

I repeated this exercise two more times – leaving the room, coming back in, sitting down at the computer, doing my energy reboot, then a 1-minute work task.

The next morning, when I came to my computer to start work, I suddenly noticed a moment of choice before checking email — I realized I was now *consciously aware* for a few seconds and could *choose* to do my Energy Reboot Practice in that moment.

I had successfully inserted a conscious moment of choice within a pattern of behavior that had been habitual and instinctual for thousands of days. And this was all with a few minutes of intentional practice!

This is an exciting idea — any behavior you want to change, you can, by doing the following:

Step 1: Decide on the new behavior.
Step 2: Practice it in the context where it usually happens.
Step 3: Repeat that practice 3 times in a row.

You will have inserted a new moment of choice into what was previously your autopilot or instinctual response.

Another example:

When I walked into the kitchen, I was used to opening the snack cupboard and eating some junk food. It had become habitual.

With deliberate practice for a few minutes, I broke the pattern:

I practiced walking into the kitchen, right past the snack cupboard, and instead opened the refrigerator and got a carrot. Then I put it back and walked out of the kitchen.

I repeated this 3 times.

Next time I wanted to snack, I felt that conscious moment of choice. By intentionally choosing the healthier option, I began to solidify a better habit.

One final example:

When I pick up my phone, I naturally want to go and surf social media and can lose track of time.

Deliberate practice: Pick up the phone, open the Calendar app, and think for a moment about my next task. (For leisure, open the Kindle app and read a book for a minute.) Put down the phone. Then repeat that exercise 3 times. I have now broken an unhelpful instinct and will begin a new behavior, thanks to intentional repetition.

Conscious practice can create any new way of being.

Using this technique, even fear can be dispelled.

The psychologist Albert Bandura conducted laboratory studies demonstrating that someone with a fear of snakes can, through gradual exposure, lose that fear, handling snakes with no problem! This is all done without hypnosis.

The phobic patients began by watching movies of other people who are calm when handling snakes. That made them more open to starting the progressive exposure to snakes, which led to overcoming their fear completely.

This can work for you as well:

When you think of a task you dislike, such as taxes, could you imagine — see a movie in your mind — a Zen-like master approaching their taxes with a mindful breath, even a joyful ease?

This is something I have actually practiced: Opening my spreadsheet for doing taxes, consciously breathing and putting a gentle smile on my face, and intentionally being grateful for each line item, thinking about the importance or necessity of each item, even marveling at it.

Here are the steps for overcoming negative emotional associations of any task:

Step 1: Imagine (or write down if it's easier) a scene in which you are doing the task without any negative emotions, but instead, doing it in a way that you would enjoy: with a mindful breath, a gentle smile, a sincere appreciation of the opportunity to do that task, marveling at the details, or in joyful service to your growth and to the greater whole.

Step 2: Intentionally practice that behavior and mindset now.

Step 3: Repeat the practice at least 3 times.

Again, you are using the power of repetition to create an emotional muscle memory for how you approach the task.

In this way, you can change your relationship to any activity you "have to" do, into one that you can actually enjoy.

- Perhaps you've wanted to make regular videos like I do, but you're steeped in self-criticism and perfectionism. Practice by pressing the Record button, then consciously replacing any negative emotion with something you would enjoy, perhaps a feeling of genuine connection to a caring audience member, or perhaps a sense of adventure in the journey of your growth.

- Perhaps you've been meaning to contact some potential clients but you're anxious and fearful about rejection, even though you know that if you do contact them, some of them are likely to hire or refer you. Practice starting the contacting process and replacing any negative emotion with something you'd enjoy... perhaps imagining how grateful they (or someone they know) would be to hear that your service exists.

Again, it is possible to change your relationship to any task that you wish to do more consistently... to be able to do it with joy!

This can replace the idea of "discipline" if you haven't loved that word.

Instead of powering or hustling through a project with unpleasant feelings, use intentional practice to change your feelings about that task. As you've seen from all the above examples, even 3 minutes can start to change a habitual pattern.

You are a bundle of habits, of muscle memory, both physical and emotional. Whatever you think you "are", you can be radically different – if you are willing to practice a new way.

Just 3 minutes can set you on a new path. You are truly flexible and can become anything you passionately set your mind to.

The key is to keep returning to the practice.

To watch the companion video or comment on this chapter, go here: www.bit.ly/jpv2c12

13. When You're Feeling "Not Ready" to Put Your Work Out There...

I see many aspiring business owners doing this:

Waiting until they're "ready" before taking the leap.

A dear client asked me about the "thin line between readiness and procrastination."

After coaching hundreds of business owners, I can tell you this:

Chances are, you are being fooled by your own brilliant mind. Feeling of "lack of readiness" is usually procrastination.

Here's the truth:

I rarely feel "ready."

When I started writing this chapter, I felt maybe I wouldn't have enough to say... maybe I should do more research or journaling or give it a few more days (or weeks) before I'm ready to start writing.

When making a video — at the moment I press "record" I feel like I could've spent another hour thinking about the topic.

When I launch a course, I know I could spend several more months (or years!) researching the topic... but I remind myself that whatever I *already* know will be helpful to the students. We are usually much harsher on ourselves than our students / clients are.

The founder of Linkedin, Reid Hoffman, famously said this:

If you're not embarrassed by the first version of your product, you've launched too late.

I feel embarrassed often... because I create often.

Every book that I publish I feel slightly embarrassed by... but the reality is that if I waited until a book was "ready" I might never publish. Thankfully I do publish, because book after book, each one is getting better. I can always re-publish and re-launch the next edition later... and I am already planning for it!

Every course that I teach, I'm embarrassed by, but I also get feedback that makes the course better, year after year.

I'm doing this for the long term journey of growth, not just short-term experiences of posting, publishing, launching.

The creative process, the reality of building an authentic business, requires this continual practice:

Transform fear into Love.

I feel that we are being called by Spirit to recognize when we are feeling afraid in the creative process and to instead reinterpret that emotion. Turn "fear" or "lack of readiness" into one or more of these:

- Excitement

- Passion
- Service
- Curious self-exploration
- Adventure

Transform hesitation into Action.

If I am creating something, and I feel hesitation, I now interpret it as a signal to take action, to just do it. To take the next step. To write the next sentence. To click "record" on the video. To press "publish."

Transform embarrassment into Surrender.

After putting your work out there, you may feel embarrassed by it and want to delete it. Don't.

Practice surrendering to the process and you'll grow a bit stronger, more confident, each time.

I recently had this kind of experience: being embarrassed by something I put out there, and after confessing my feelings about it (while *not* deleting the embarrassing thing), I found that people didn't judge me the way I had judged myself.

Transmuting fearful hesitation into loving action and surrendering to the process is a daily creative process. Bit by bit, piece by piece, we become more courageous. We get wiser through action and experience.

A little-known fact is that the creative person's doubt and "lack of readiness" never goes away. We simply get better at recognizing it and transmuting it into creative action.

So there's only one thing to do:

Start today.

Bias yourself toward action, doing what you are afraid of, knowing that it can be interpreted as excitement, passion, service. Go ahead and write, speak, publish, launch, ... do the thing that puts your work into the marketplace.

To watch the companion video or comment on this chapter, go here: www.bit.ly/jpv2c13

14. Get Unstuck by Asking Smaller Questions

Have you ever felt stuck trying to answer **big** questions such as. . .

- "What is my niche?"
- "Who is my ideal client?"
- "What's my marketing message?"
- "What's my Calling in life?!"

These questions carry a finality that can overwhelm us. It's like once you answer it, you lose your flexibility.

"The decision would affect so many little things!"

"Therefore I can't move forward until I've figured it all out!"

It's no wonder that many of us procrastinate on growing our business. These big questions can keep us stuck for years.

A wise mentor once said to me:

Our calling can only be understood when looking *backward*.

Observing the twists and turns of your life, you can start to connect the dots – to see the pattern of your previous opportunities, the people you happened to meet, your successes, and what you learned from your so-called "failures."

By connecting the dots of our past, we start to understand our Calling.

And yet, Life is lived forward.

Are we going in the "right" direction? Yes, planning helps prevent mistakes, but when it's something complex (and ever-evolving) such as our authentic business, there are too many factors we aren't aware of, for which we cannot plan.

"We plan, and God laughs..."—Yiddish proverb

We don't really know how we will personally evolve, or how society's surprising changes may affect our future decisions. Therefore, the wisest way to build an authentic business, and to discover our calling, is to take the stance of experimentation.

"All life is an experiment. The more experiments you make the better." Ralph Waldo Emerson

From a more playful perspective, let us reframe those big intimidating questions...

"What's my niche?" can be reframed as:

"What's the next niche I'd like to explore, through experimentation?"

Instead of the false finality of "defining" my niche, I am always testing new ideas, while doubling-down on recent ideas that got traction.

For example, years ago I noticed that I was answering many questions from my audience about Facebook Ads. So I decided to test out that niche by teaching a single 2-hour workshop on that topic.

People loved it!

So I repeated it, this time for a colleague's audience. They loved it too.

Now, my Facebook Marketing Course is what many people know me for. In the minds of those people, that's George Kao's "niche."

(I don't care how people define me—as long as they find benefit from my work. In fact, I don't mind being pigeonholed.)

Another example:

I was interested in the topic of healthy money (relating to money in a wiser way), so I tried writing some articles about it. Most of those received lackluster responses. Therefore, it's not a niche that I'll be putting much effort into. If it were a hobby, I might keep writing about it—I guess that's why I kept it up so long. However, for business, I'd rather focus on ideas that get a better market response!

"Who's my ideal audience?" can be reframed as:

"Who has recently been responding to my authentic content?"

or. . .

"What group of people will I try advertising my content to next?"

This is why I preach the message of creating authentic content: in your content, be yourself (don't try to be like anyone else.) Talk about your passions, talk about what has helped you and others you know, and then observe who responds to your authenticity.

You can also make experiments by running Facebook Ads to different audiences and see if they like your content.

Then, as you start offering your products and services, observe who buys. That's the beginning of your true ideal audience. Study who your buyers are.

When I started my business more than 10 years ago, I imagined that my ideal audience looked like me: 30's male, business school graduate. Yet as I created content and started to enroll clients, I was surprised: my audience was mostly women, and many of them were in their 50's, mostly without business degrees.

That taught me an important lesson: Instead of trying to define my ideal audience, let them reveal themselves to me over time.

"What should my product/service be?" can be reframed as:

"What have I already been helping people with?"

or. . .

"What will I try helping people with next?"

We often take for granted the skills we use to help others.

Whatever we do skillfully is so "obvious" or "normal" to us, that we don't appreciate the value it brings to others.

It's like a fish teaching a monkey to swim: it's no big deal for the fish, but it's a huge revelation for the monkey!

If you start noticing the skills you use to help others, you'll find clues for your next experimental product or service. (Start keeping track of what problems others ask your advice on, and what you're spending time helping others with.)

"What's my marketing message?" can be reframed as...

"What headline would I like to test next?"

or...

"What sales page shall I draft next?"

It's intimidating (even for marketing experts like me) to think of a single unifying marketing message.

Truthfully, you don't have just "one" message.

Every single product/service has its own marketing message.

Over time, as you create content and observe the reactions of your audience, your overarching Core Message will become clearer to you.

Until then, just focus on experimenting in your content, playing with the various passions you have, sharing what's on your mind, and testing the message of your next offering.

Until it becomes obvious, stay flexible.

Information about ourselves, society, and our audience gets updated, at an increasingly faster pace.

Building our authentic business is a highly complex project, and it is fantasy to try to plan far into the future and still remain authentic in the moment.

It is both more realistic, and authentic, to just experiment with the next thing.

Your future direction is beyond your current understanding.

Allow your Calling to be understood backward, and simply live forward with playful experimentation, the curiosity of a scientist or artist!

To make progress now, ask yourself a small question:

"What's the next thing I'd like to try?"

To watch the companion video or comment on this chapter, go here: www.bit.ly/jpv2c14

15. Green, Yellow, Red

One of the secrets to a joyfully productive life:

Learn to become sensitive – often – to your state of being, throughout the day.

And if you catch yourself in a less-than-optimal state, do your energy reboot practice, right away, to re-enter a good state.

A simple way to gauge your state of being is to ask:

"Right now, am I in green, red, or yellow?"

Green = feeling deeply peaceful or happy. When I'm working, Green means being in flow, confident, skillful, curious. When I'm resting, Green has me feeling nourished.

Red = feeling exhausted and negative, easily giving into addiction. Feelings may include anxiety, fear, sadness, hopelessness, overwhelm, anger.

Yellow = the most important state to become sensitive to: the boundary state between Green and Red.

By practicing awareness of your internal state throughout the day, you create more choice. You're more able to maintain flow and balance, no matter what you're doing.

Green: Flow

When you're green, and working, then you are being joyfully productive.

If you are doing something you know how to do, then Green means you're confident, empowered, and in service to your higher purpose.

If it's something challenging, then Green means you are in the mode of exploration and learning. You are playfully curious.

Take a moment and think about the last time you felt green.

The more you can become aware of your Green state, the more often you'll find yourself there. We tend to subconsciously create what we consciously notice.

Notice when you are in Green today.

Green is not about the activity you're doing. You can be in Green when doing any useful activity, no matter how "boring" or challenging.

Your state of being is habituated based on practice, which is your choice.

Red: Negativity

This is when you are desperately needing recovery and balance.

Hopefully you will rarely allow yourself to get into the Red zone.

This is where relationships with others become strained. It's where we start going into addiction. It's where we quit our work due to frustration or overwhelm and exhaustion.

When in Red, we make short-term decisions based on impulsive negative emotions. We are also easily manipulatable because we're not grounded in our authentic power.

I hope we'll do our best to never go back into Red.

Yet how did we get to Red in the first place? It's because we weren't sensitive to the Yellow state. . . .

Yellow: Boundary

This is the boundary between GREEN (flow and balance) and RED (unhealthy emotions).

Yellow is important. It is a warning.

Do you know when you are in Yellow? Most people haven't practiced recognizing it. Mindfulness is required to become sensitive to this state.

Practice checking in with yourself frequently. At least once every waking hour – ideally many times – take 5 seconds to ask yourself: "Am I in Green, Yellow, or Red?"

Practice until you are able to describe your Yellow:

- When you are no longer in Green, and heading towards Red, what does it feel like?

- What type of situations trigger your Yellow? (With practice, you'll eventually be able to stay in Green almost all the time, but in the beginning it's useful to know what situations trigger your Yellow.)

- What activities bring you into Yellow?

- What time of day tends to find you in Yellow?

Become increasingly clear about your Yellow, so you can catch yourself sooner and bring yourself back to Green.

You always have a choice.

Tools for Getting Back to Green

The first step is consistent awareness of what state you're in.

The second step is to do the activity that helps you to recover.

Such activities are different for different people, so you'll need to discover what works for you.

These tools help me stay in Green:

Energy Reboot

Whenever I catch myself in Yellow (or Red), I immediately take a moment to take an easy, deep breath.

Then I do what I call an Energy Reboot.

For some people, tapping (EFT) can be enormously helpful. If so, be sure to use it regularly!

Evening/Morning Routine

Having a well-designed and consistent evening routine so I get enough sleep, and a morning routine that makes me feel great about starting the day.

This means being diligent to end my workday on time, so that I can have the evening focused on relaxation and renewal.

Most of us tend to be in "work" mode too often. We may not have planned enough guilt-free "down time". (Ironically, for many of us, it does take planning to carve out enough free time to ourselves!) Without enough recovery, we cannot be as focused and effective. My evenings as well as Sundays are my "planned" down-time from work.

It's not that I "never" do work at those times, but it's rare, and I never feel any obligation.

During the down-times, I aim to have as much "boredom" as I can, because that means I truly have nothing planned, I'm completely free to do whatever I want. That is helpful for renewal and refreshment of our mind.

Scheduled Breaks

I stick to my scheduled breaks each work day:

- 10:00-11:30am Dog-walk, breakfast, nap
- 1-2pm Light lunch and nap
- 4:30-6pm Snack, nap, and dog-walk

My naps are about 20 minutes, where I simply lie down, relax, and breathe with good thoughts. Occasionally I fall asleep, but even if I don't, it feels good to just lie down for awhile.

Ambient Tools

I call these ambient tools because they can be with us all the time:

- Deep, gentle breaths
- Gentle smiling
- Small quick stretch

Some people may find soft/instrumental music helpful. Maybe also aromatherapy (candle or essential oils).

Are there other tools that help you move into or stay in Green? Comment below and share with us.

Commit to Awareness of Your State

Again, the first step is awareness. Commit to becoming mindful, many moments of each day, about whether you are in Green, Yellow, or Red.

When I'm working, I usually check in with my state every 10 minutes or so. Sometimes 40 minutes go by and I catch myself having forgotten to check in. That's ok. I appreciate that I caught myself, and gently do an energy reboot.

Commit to the daily practice of the tools that bring you back to Green.

When people are in Green, wonderful things happen in the world. There's kindness, optimism, and confidence, and good things get done.

When people are in Red, there's stuckness, wallowing, and violence – emotional, psychological, physical.

Let's change the world by helping each other notice Green, Yellow, Red. Let's help each other move into Green more often.

Of course, we must start with ourselves.

Consider sharing this message. Help make the world a Greener place

To watch the companion video or comment on this chapter, go here: www.bit.ly/jpv2c15

16. Uninspired but Willing

I share this "secret" with many creators: I don't feel inspired until I've *already* started creating.

I often feel uninspired. But I am willing to try.

It's how I start my work most of the time. This very piece you're reading started with an uninspired mood.

Working conditions don't seem ideal to me most of the time:

I'm either not feeling like doing what my schedule says...

Or there's construction or other noise going on...

Or I'm not in the mood for thinking about this project.

As a result, I've had lots of practice working in suboptimal conditions. Because that is almost always the case.

Yet, ideas for projects can appear at any time. Walking the dog. Taking a shower. Working on another project. The few times that inspiration does strike, I take a moment to write it down on my phone. (In the shower, I memorize the idea and immediately write it down after I finish showering.)

I give thanks for those moments of clarity. But honestly, it's less than 5% of a typical day.

Most of the day, you'll find me simply, humbly following my schedule. If it's my scheduled time to write, I try to write. When I begin, I'm not inspired, but I write anyway, starting with an idea that was given to me (by inspiration) sometime in the past. (As I mentioned, it helps to keep a list of ideas.)

Most of the day, I have to practice generating flow on demand.

What does help – gives me the faith to continue despite lack of inspiration – is my Energy Reboot, which I do before starting any work session. It takes 30 seconds. Therefore, it's easy to do often.

The great composer Tchaikovsky said:

"I sit down to the piano regularly at nine-o'clock in the morning and The Lady Muses have learned to be on time for that rendezvous."

Dutch journalist Peter R. de Vries said: "I only write when I am inspired. And I see to it that I am inspired at 9 a.m. every morning."

Interesting that they both say 9am.

When I first began to write (trying to overcome writer's block), I wrote at night, right before bed. That worked well for 6 months.

Then, I experimented with writing in the morning, which worked well for several years.

Now, since about 2 years ago, I've been writing in the afternoons, and it seems to work just as well.

So perhaps it doesn't really matter what time of day? What matters more is one's commitment and follow-through.

With ongoing experience in an activity, we grow confidence. With mindfulness brought to our actions, we grow skill.

The celebrated painter Chuck Close said:

"The advice I like to give young artists, or really anybody who'll listen to me, is not to wait around for inspiration. **Inspiration is for amateurs; the rest of us just show up and get to work.** *If you wait around for the clouds to part and a bolt of lightning to strike you in the brain, you are not going to make an awful lot of work. All the best ideas come out of the process; they come out of the work itself. Things occur to you. If you're sitting around trying to dream up a great art idea, you can sit there a long time before anything happens. But if you just get to work, something will occur to you and something else will occur to you and something else that you reject will push you in another direction.* **Inspiration is absolutely unnecessary and somehow deceptive.** *You feel like you need this great idea before you can get down to work, and I find that's almost never the case."* [Emphasis added.]

More than 1,000 videos and blog posts later, I can confirm from experience that what is written above is true for me as well.

When I am first writing a blog post, I don't know how it is going to turn out. Often, I cannot easily see how I will write more than a few sentences about the topic.

Sometimes I'm already halfway through my writing session, and I regret starting. "I chose the wrong topic!" But my schedule says that I need to finish the blog post in half an hour... so I keep going.

I've never regretted continuing and publishing, even if I didn't think it was worth publishing.

I write and publish on schedule, usually not feeling like it when I begin, but always feeling glad afterwards.

That's when I know I'm following my purpose, and experiencing growth – working through creative discomfort, doing it anyway, and then feeling good at the end.

"Being a professional is doing the things you love to do, on the days you don't feel like doing them." – Julius Erving, basketball legend.

"I don't wait for moods. You accomplish nothing if you do that. Your mind must know it has to get down to work." – Pearl Buck, celebrated Novelist.

If you are committed to creating, you've got to *question your discomfort and uncertainty* during the very act of work. It's normal to doubt that we can do it. It's fine to be baffled by where the direction is supposed to go with any creative piece.

Always remember the normality of creative discomfort. We all experience it, at every stage of the game.

I feel the same discomfort today that I did years ago when I started writing. The key difference is that now I've experienced, again and again, the necessity of working through it.

To watch the companion video or comment on this chapter, go here: www.bit.ly/jpv2c16

17. Capture, Categorize, Calendar

A reader asked:

"How do I stay on top of my big volume of tasks and not feel overwhelmed?"

I recommend that you think of tasks and information just like physical clutter: how do you solve that problem? Everything important goes into the right place. (What's not important should be given away or recycled/trashed.) Then create a system for reminding yourself where the important stuff is.

Similarly, here is how I organize my ideas, my wishes, my don't-forget-to's, and everything else that's important:

Capture > Categorize > Calendar

In other words:

- Write down what seems important.
- Park it in a system.
- Have a reminder to work on it at the appropriate time.

This is an idea I borrowed from David Allen's famous book <u>Getting Things Done</u>.

Without a system, it is easy to be in constant overwhelm, trying to keep everything in our head and wondering when we'll finally get to work on important things. Even new ideas can be the source of anxiety.

Capture > Categorize > Calendar ... This practice ends the question of "When are you going to work on this?"

Follow this system and you will never again feel like something might fall through the cracks. It is a system I've relied on completely for 10 years to build a successful business, maintain good health and enjoy family life.

Step 1: Capture

Our brains are terrible storage devices. Instead, they are wonderful for pattern recognition, improvisation, relationships, and problem solving... but not in the accuracy of recall.

"The palest ink is more reliable than the most powerful memory."
–Chinese Proverb

Albert Einstein himself wouldn't bother to remember his own phone number. He didn't want to waste his brain on recalling details. When we try to remember something, we are using precious mental resources that can be used for relating, creating, or processing ideas subconsciously.

Want a more efficient brain? Write down what's important so you don't have to remember it!

I have multiple documents where I write down my processes, and I refer to them frequently. One example is <u>my daily reviews</u>.

Capture all your ideas as they arrive. Then work with them later.

The very moment of thinking of an idea, a task, a problem, can create a feeling that it is important right now.

That's an illusion. Very few things are actually urgent, but the immediacy of an idea deceives us into thinking that it is.

Instead, remember this:

Distance creates perspective.

Any idea that comes to you in the moment, a task you might want to do, new information, new challenges... if it feels important, simply put it into its proper time and place to later integrate or solve.

Capture all your ideas first... and then work with them later.

Even in the shower, I capture ideas. I use AquaNotes.

Everywhere else, I capture them into my Todoist app. I first capture new ideas into the "Today" category. Then at the end of the day, I categorize everything from the Today category into their own categories, so that Today gets cleared out.

One of the main reasons people are anxious and unable to complete projects is that they allow themselves to be driven by internal whims and external demands... getting blown about here and there... not living by a self-generated, long-term purpose.

Imagine responding to every single email as it comes in! (I hope you don't!) Instead, you know it is more efficient if you let them collect in your inbox, and then deal with them as a batch. Similarly, capture your ideas in order to action them at the proper time.

Practice capturing your ideas all throughout the day.

1. What tool will you use to capture your ideas? Pick something that you can have with you at all times, whether it's Todoist, Google Keep, or just a small pad of paper that you write on.

2. Practice capturing ideas throughout the day, for 1 week.

3. If you'd like to report on how things go for you, add a comment below, sharing which tool you chose, and how it felt to practice capturing your ideas.

(As mentioned, I use Todoist – if you want to try it, but you're already using another tool system, just google "import from [your current tool] into Todoist" and there will be an article or video showing you how.)

Step 2: Categorize

Once or twice a day, move your tasks and ideas from the "inbox" or "today" (where you have been capturing them) into a proper "category" that you can work with later.

In Todoist, a category is called a Project. I recommend keeping it simple, and don't use tags until you first master the practice of categorizing things into Projects.

If you don't use a task management system, you can simply capture your ideas in a blank Google Doc, and then categorize them into different Google Docs based on projects (by cutting-and-pasting them over).

You need to define what categories are important to you, what "projects" you are working on. In my business, I use these categories:

- Video Ideas

- Workshops

- Client Groups

- Service Improvement

- Admin

- Book

- Networking

- Marketing Optimization

- Content

Or a much simpler example:

- Marketing

- Client Services

- Administration

Consider your categories to be your "big rocks". If you've never heard that time management parable before, check it out here: www.bitly.com/coveybigrocks

I do my categorization once at the beginning of my day, and once at the end of my day.

Here's how I do it:

1. Can this idea / task be eliminated? Most of us try to do too many tasks, cluttering up our time very quickly. For each task, ask: Does the idea bring me joy, or truly make something else easier, or will significantly help someone? If not, eliminate it.

2. If I can't eliminate it, then I put it into a Category and remove the due date. Whenever I log an idea into Todoist, I put it in the "Today" category so that it automatically has the due-date of today. At the end of each day I categorize any remaining

ideas for the day (putting them into their appropriate Projects) and remove the due dates.

3. If it's so important that I don't want to risk forgetting about it, I put a future due date on it, so it pops back up into my awareness at a later time. (However, if you do the next step of Calendaring, you will always have time to look back at the ideas you've categorized.)

Step 3: Calendar

Put into your Calendar every single "category" you have: for example, schedule time for content creation, for client administration, etc.

If you calendar your categories, then no project can fall through the cracks. Your calendar is your assistant, so let it assist you!

If you never calendar in your Marketing, for example, your business may never have enough visibility. (I schedule time each week to create content. The articles and videos don't make themselves!)

I use Google Calendar for this step.

It's free and reliable. I've been using it for my business and life for more than a decade. There's also a corresponding app on iPhone and Android.

This means when the time arrives in my Calendar to work on a Category, I simply open up the corresponding project/notebook, and then work on what's important at that time.

Here's the key – You don't have to do things in order. Once you are working on your Category (Project) and looking at a list of tasks or ideas in there, allow your intuition to guide you to the task that feels most inspiring and energizing in that moment and focus on that.

In other words, be left-brained and logical when you are Categorizing and Calendaring. But when the actual time for action arrives, open your list of ideas/tasks for that category, and then be right-brained and intuitive about it, doing from that list whatever feels right.

Example of using Capture, Categorize, Calendar...

I have an idea right now. I want to add a new feature to my Client Group. I'm excited about it. Do I set aside everything I planned today and work on this new feature? No... instead, I use Capture, Categorize, Calendar.

I take a moment to capture the idea by writing it down into my Todoist "Today" category.

Then at the end of the day, I categorize it into my project called "Client Group".

I also make sure that I have time scheduled in my calendar to work on "Client Group".

When the time arrives on my calendar to work on "Client Group", I work on the new feature/idea I was thinking about. By then, the idea will be more refined because my subconscious has been working on it for days.

When you write down an idea, your subconscious mind starts working on it right away, even when you aren't consciously thinking about it. By the time you get around to working on that idea, you'll have the benefit of a more refined idea. Distance creates perspective!

You can also enjoy the anticipation. It's like when you plan a trip somewhere, you experience the pleasure of thinking about it, looking forward to it. This can be true of any ideas you write down. You can enjoy anything, if you intend to!

Back to the importance of Calendaring – If I don't schedule a time to work on a project, that category often gets neglected.

This is how I organize everything:
Capture > Categorize > Calendar.

Go ahead and try it out. Any questions, feel free to let me know.

I look forward to hearing about your progress! Let me know how you are applying this practice, and how your life/business improves as a result.

To watch the companion video or comment on this chapter, go here: www.bit.ly/jpv2c17

18. Stop "Preparing" So Much... Break the Pattern of Delay

A common thought pattern that prevents a lot of people from making progress in their business:

Before I... [take the next real step in my business]
... I need to first do
[some preparatory action that takes a lot of time]
... so that I'll feel more ready/confident to move forward.

This is a dangerous train of thought because "preparation" always sounds logical... until you wake up to the fact that you have already been preparing for months (maybe years!)... and you can be in preparation mode for the rest of your life.

Here are some ways that "preparation mode" often shows up:

"I just need to get this one more training, this additional certification... then I'll be ready."

Truth:

There will always be another training or certification being sold to you, that you "must" take in order to feel confident and finally ready.

This is what marketers (and learning institutions) tend to do — create gaps in your mind, the fear of missing out (FOMO) and the fear of failure if you don't sign up for their training.

True learning happens through action in the real world. Too many trainings are about knowledge transfer from "expert" to student, rather than witnessing and guiding the students to take action in real time.

Honestly, most of you reading this have gotten enough training to do your work. By actually helping people (starting with your friends) with the skills you wish to be an expert at, you will learn more than consuming yet another course or book.

"I first need to develop fool-proof clarity about my framework... then I can create and share content with the world. I don't want to embarrass myself by having to publicly revise my ideas later."

You will find that your framework, as you start to develop it, is so expansive and deep – and ever evolving – that it is not something you'll be able to *completely* understand and describe *before* you get out there and share what you know.

New understanding will always be unfolding, and therefore, revisions of previous knowledge are inevitable.

Trying to get to "the right idea" before you start publicly sharing your knowledge means that you will be in preparation mode for the rest of your life.

I started teaching in 2009 before I had what I'd now call a "framework". I just taught what I understood at the time, what I had already found to be helpful. Who appreciated and benefited from what I knew? People who understood even less than me.

There will always be people who understand less than you, who would benefit from whatever experience you *already* have, without you having to learn more first.

As I kept learning from real-world experience, I eventually created my framework and I keep updating it (to this day), each time teaching what is true for me in that moment.

Again, there are always people who can benefit from what you *already* know. Just start talking, teaching, and sharing your knowledge. That is actually the best, real way to learn – by observing other people's reactions to whatever it is that you share in the moment.

"I need to wait until my kids are older... I just need to wait until my parents no longer need my caretaking... then I will build my business."

It is true that any kind of caretaking, whether for children, parents, or someone else, takes an enormous amount of energy.

Yet, I have clients with young kids, or aging parents, who consistently carve out time to do productive actions to build their business. I'm so proud of them, that they simply try to show up each week with at least a few hours put into their businesses.

Don't wait. Just carve out a sliver of time each week to take real action. Don't let your family be an excuse to delay your business. Otherwise, you may end up blaming them later.

"I need to fully update my website... then I'll be ready to share about my business, create and distribute content, reach out for promotional partners, do my launch, etc..."

No matter how much time and money you spend on it, you will always feel that your website can be improved.

Typically, you can just launch – when you have a new offering to share – with a particular landing page having been updated, since that's where the vast majority of traffic will go anyway. Read about it: why you might only need a one-page website.

Unless you're getting consistent comments from people about a specific thing that you *must* change on your website, it is better to look at your website as a work-in-progress-forever, and just keep making small improvements even as you take action to market specific aspects of your business.

There are plenty of things I can do to improve my website, but I just keep sharing content, sending newsletters, reaching out for potential promotional partners, doing launches, etc... and gradually make improvements to my website along the way.

Don't be afraid of mistakes, nor missed opportunities.

Being "perfect" is an illusion. You already know and have enough to take real action.

Break your pattern of delay.

Do the real actions that are needed to build your business:

1. Consistently let your network know, in a direct way, that your business exists, and what your current offering is. Do this through social media, email newsletters (if any), and personal outreach.

2. Publicly share what you already know in your field, so that you can educate and grow your audience. Do this by consistently posting authentic content. Do this on so-

cial media, and if you have email subscribers, send a newsletter once a month.

3. Consistently be reaching out to potential promotional partners, colleagues you might enjoy collaborating with. You could cross-promote each other's content or offerings, for example.

As you look at your schedule for the week or month, be concerned if a large portion of your time will be spent in "learning" or preparation mode.

Break the pattern of delay!

Decide today to spend the majority of your working hours doing the things that actually move your business forward.

To determine what those things are for you, refer back to Chapter 4: True Productivity.

To watch the companion video or comment on this chapter, go here: www.bit.ly/jpv2c18

19. My Top 5 Motivational Methods

If a goal is challenging (and the most worthwhile goals are!), you will need motivational methods that are effective for you personally. You'll need to continually practice the methods that help you focus and make progress, so you can get through it no matter how "hard" the task feels.

Below, I describe the methods that have worked best for me and my clients.

As you read this, I invite you to score each method on a scale of 0 to 10. Zero means "I've tried many times and this doesn't work for me" and 10 means "This is a game-changer for me!"

Here are the 5 methods:

1. Write down the baby steps

When I find myself procrastinating, I do this:

1. Write down what is the thing I'm trying to accomplish. For example "Write a blog post."

2. Write down the baby steps – very doable action steps. For example:

a. In a blank document, brainstorm 3 points that I'd like to make in the post.

b. Write a few sentences about each point.

c. Rearrange and edit the sentences.

3. If any step feels daunting, chunk that down into even more granular steps: e.g. "Brainstorm 3 points" can be chunked down to the question *"What's 1 thing that I feel is true about this topic?"* and after I answer that question, then *"What's another thing that's true about it?"*

When I look at the list of steps and I think *"Oh I can definitely do this, if I just follow the steps,"* then I know I've chunked it down enough to make it doable.

4. Take a moment and "see" myself doing the actions with <u>calm joyful focus</u>. . . "I see myself typing ideas about this topic, with a gentle smile on my face."

And then I get started right away on the first small action step. (Even if I only have time for that first little step, at least I have become unstuck!)

To take this method even further, try setting a tiny deadline for each of the various steps. Example:

a. Open a blank document – 2:01pm

b. Brainstorm 3 points that I'd like to make in the post – 2:10pm

c. Write a few sentences about each point – 2:30pm

d. Rearrange and edit the sentences – 2:50pm

What project is important to you, but that you find yourself procrastinating on?

Try this method – chunking things down to very next actions that feel doable for you.

2. Five minute method

I remind myself:

I can do anything for 5 minutes.

I set a timer for 5 minutes, and make any progress on the project I've been putting off. (Perhaps the time will be spent writing down the baby steps.)

It doesn't have to be brilliant. Just any progress is helpful for now.

Here's the key:

Before I start the timer, I take a moment to place myself in a positive state of mind, by doing my energy reboot practice.

If I am creating something for my audience, then I will also do this: Bring to mind an ideal audience member. It might be a current client, or a reader who comments supportively on my posts.

I imagine that person in front of me, eagerly waiting for me to create this project because it will help them. The key is to bring to mind/heart a person for whom I can do no wrong in their eyes: a true fan.

(Of course, no real human being can be 100% perfectly supportive without mistake, but in this temporary imagination, they are allowed to be perfectly supportive!)

Once I'm in this heart-based mindset, I will start the 5 minute timer and make any progress I can in that time.

What might I actually do in that time? Options include:

- Brainstorming the steps needed for this project
- Writing my first draft
- Organizing my ideas
- Recording an initial video
- Reaching out to one or two people for help

I've learned that the landscape changes with every step I make, so it's more important to simply take a step so that I can see, with a bit more clarity, what is next.

After the 5 minutes are complete, I take a break and celebrate a bit.

Or, if I am on a roll, I will keep going for another 20-45 minutes!

If I do take a break, though, I can always come back and do another 5 minutes, using this same method.

This 5-minute technique has unblocked me, and many of my clients, in our projects.

Try it and let me know if this helps you too.

3. Co-Working

If you are needing some accountability to create content, try content co-working.

For all types of work, I use this strangely effective online tool: Focusmate.

If I'm not in a meeting with clients, or on a break, then I am on Focusmate. Yes, several hours every working day!

The way it works is simple – you get paired up with someone else (online) who wants to work at the same time. At the beginning, you check-in for a minute about what project you're working on, and then each person quietly works until the end of the hour, and then you briefly check in again at the end.

That's it.

(In fact, I'm on a focusmate session right now as I'm typing this!)

This simple accountability method has supported me as I've written 4 books, created dozens of online courses, and built a thriving business.

If you haven't tried it, give it at least 3 sessions. It just might change your life, as it has for me and many of my clients.

Part of why it works so well is that by scheduling Focusmate sessions, you are scheduling an appointment and someone is counting on you to be there, and yet during the appointment, you get to focus on what's important to you.

Join Focusmate. I hope to see you there!

4. Accountability Partner

This is about having one Accountability Partner for at least 1 month at a time.

Research has shown that when you write down your goals and action commitments, and then share them with an Accountability Partner, and then report back to your partner, the average increase in productivity is 77%. Check out the research here.

An accountability partner could be:

- Coach
- Friend

- Colleague
- A kindred spirit from a course or an online community

Meet once a week for 15-30 minutes. Or when something is really important, you might even meet daily. The accountability can go both ways – each person reports on their project. If you can't schedule time to talk, then message with them once a week or more often.

A simple format for accountability meetings:

1. What progress has been made since the last time we talked?
2. Did you accomplish what you said you would? If not, how will you ensure that you complete it? If you did complete it, what will you do by our next call?
3. What state of being do you want to be in / what is the attitude or spirit you'll embody as you do the project?

You could even consider having multiple accountability partners, if each person can only meet with you once a month or once a week, and you want accountability more often.

After the call, send your action commitment to your accountability partner. Expect them to send theirs (if they are also needing accountability from you). Again, the research shows that by doing this action, people accomplish 77% more.

5. Public event promising a deliverable

The more people expecting you to do something, the more likely you'll do it.

With this method of public accountability, you announce a deliverable with a specific deadline to your network/audience.

You'll likely complete it by the deadline, so you don't embarrass yourself! :)

This method is not for everybody, but it has worked extraordinarily well for me. Along with Focusmate, public accountability keeps me on track to create courses, launch books, and other accomplishments in my business over the years.

Here's a simple way to do it:

Go to Facebook Events – on that page you'll find the "create new event" button on the left side. Create an event with the date/time being the deadline for accomplishing your project. Invite your friends and ask for their support. Along the way, post on that event page with your progress.

This can work really well if you are creating content for an online course, a webinar, a presentation, a book, or updating your website.

Announce something you believe is doable, but just a bit of a stretch. Not something that will stress you out, but will feel challenging to you in a good way.

**

There you have it, 5 powerful methods to keep you motivated in doing your important projects.

No matter which method you use, I wish you love as your deeper motivation: the joy and privilege of working on purpose, in service to your higher mission, knowing that all will turn out beautifully.

Your turn – comment below on which method you're excited to try.

If you have another method that works well to motivate you during challenging projects, I'd love to hear about it below.

To watch the companion video or comment on this chapter, go here: www.bit.ly/jpv2c19

20. Calm Joyful Focus

When working, are you aware of your facial expression, your body posture, your breathing?

The more challenging the project, the more tense your face and body might get. This doesn't help you to do better work. Yet it increases stress.

Years ago I started practicing what I call "calm joyful focus", which is to practice noticing, throughout the day, my body expression as I work, especially my face.

Instead of furrowed eyebrows and pursed lips, I consciously relax my face, and hold a soft, gentle smile.

In this video, I demonstrate:
www.youtube.com/watch?v=ApC9PI6MJ3E

I also notice my body posture, especially my shoulders (are they tense? relax them), my neck (is it stiff? make it a bit more flexible by moving my head a bit), and my breathing (take a deep breath now).

In this more relaxed yet focused state, I do better work because I'm more able to bring forth an energy of positivity and possibility, and decrease the potential of burnout.

As you work today, try to become conscious of your body posture at random moments, at least every 10-20 minutes, and:

- As you become conscious of your body, breathe deeply

- Relax your shoulders

- Take a moment to gently move your neck, to keep it flexible instead of stiff

- Practice a calm, smiling face

This will allow you to sustain better health as you work. It'll also infuse your work with a more peaceful and joyful energy.

For those of us who work at the computer a lot, also notice how you are typing. Are you banging on the keys? Are your hands pressed tightly to the keyboard?

Try gently resting your hands on the keyboard. Then type lightly. This will help to prevent long-term repetitive stress injury, and also keep your computer working longer.

Focus on the Process rather than the Result

An example of calm joyful focus is a martial arts master.

In Aikido, for example, they divert an opponent's force (rather than push directly against it) and as a result, the opponent falls naturally, with little effort from the master. You can see an example in this video at 31:20 — https://youtu.be/evL12aRAE7M?t=31m20s

You'll also notice that they calmly face their opponents, rather than in Hollywood movies where they might have a fierce look. In real life, whether they are practicing or fighting, the masters maintain a calm, joyful focus. See the example here — https://youtu.be/z3j0WTKAFE8

The deeper root of having a calm, joyful focus is whether your concern is on the *result*, rather than on the process of your work. . .

"I once read an interview with a coach for the U.S. Olympic archery team. He commented that the biggest problem he faced in coaching the American team was that they were fixated on their scores, or the result of their shots. It was as if they were drawing the bow and releasing the arrow only to hit the bull's-eye and earn a good score. This was in contrast to the Asian teams, who, having grown up in different cultures, were consumed in the process of properly executing the technique that led up to releasing the shot. Where the arrow hit the target was almost unimportant compared to the motion of drawing the bow correctly and releasing the shot. They viewed the result with an almost detached indifference. For them, the desired goal was a natural result of prioritizing the proper technique of drawing the bow. They operated in a completely different paradigm, and because of it, they were very difficult to beat.... The minds of the Asian archers were quiet, uncomplicated, and free from mental turmoil. The irony was that, when compared to the results-oriented Americans, the Asians were the ones who were winning. Now, U.S. sports psychologists are teaching our athletes to think along similar lines."

—from Thomas Sterner's book <u>The Practicing Mind</u>.

When you work, you can be primarily concerned with the result (perhaps be attached to it) – or alternatively, you can practice a calm, joyful focus on the process itself.

Accept and celebrate whatever you happen to accomplish by the end of that work period, unattached to the results.

I'll complete this chapter with a couple of quotes from the Bhagavad Gita...

"The meaning of Karma is in the intention. The intention behind action is what matters. Those who are motivated only by desire for the fruits of action are miserable, for they are constantly anxious about the results of what they do."

"Set thy heart upon thy work, but never on its reward."

"Perform all thy actions with mind concentrated on the Divine, renouncing attachment and looking upon success and failure with an equal eye. Spirituality implies equanimity."

To watch the companion video or comment on this chapter, go here: bit.ly/jpv2c20

21. Rest Before You Need To

I've been able to accomplish a lot in my business because I create *even when I don't feel like it* – I work on a regular rhythm. (And I honestly *don't* feel like it most of the time.)

Similarly, I've had to learn how to **rest myself before I'm tired**... to rest on a regular rhythm, whether or not I feel like it.

Several times I've nearly burned out. (Maybe I did, and eventually recovered.) Painful experiences – emotional lows, lack of motivation, lack of hope, physical exhaustion – something I hope can be prevented for others.

Now I know how important it is – for health and for a sustainable business – to rest before I need to.

If I wait till I'm really tired, I've rested too late.

The more addictive our technologies, the harder it is to remember to take breaks.

So it's more important than ever to make it a conscious practice of taking frequent breaks. To make *resting* a key discipline in our work.

The reason for our breaks isn't just a physical one, it's also to rest from the emotional and mental states of working: various degrees of tenseness.

Staying healthy – and growing strong – means to have a healthy rhythm of stretching (working) then relaxing (not working).

I have several ways to rest:

Microbreaks

For several months, I've been practicing taking a micro-break every 15-20 minutes during every work hour, and it's been very helpful to maintain joyful productivity and well-being.

My micro-break takes about 30 seconds and goes like this:

1. Taking a few deep breaths
2. ...and while I'm doing that, my hands move off the keyboard and I drop my arms to my sides, and gently close my eyes.
3. I thank God for having brought me through all the work thus far, and give thanks that I'll be brought through the rest of it. I then do a very quick energy reboot (breathing in Love, out Security, in Wisdom, out Thanks).
4. Then, I open my eyes, look into the distance and do a quick arm stretch, yawning or sighing as needed.
5. Then I finish by reminding myself of what time the next micro-break is.

To be able to do micro-breaks requires that we have **time-consciousness**: being very aware of the time. Too many of us haven't practiced this, and it gets us into trouble. We're at the computer, in a trance, for too long.

Because I glance at the clock every few minutes while I'm working, I'm aware enough to take a micro-break every 15-20 minutes.

Mid-Day Breaks

I never work more than 2 hours without taking a large break. Such breaks last 30 minutes to 2 hours. (As mentioned above, I also take many micro-breaks during those 2 hours of work.)

Two of these mid-day breaks are just 30 minutes each:

- Snack if I need to.
- 15-minute nap. (I usually don't fall asleep, but simply relaxing, laying down, helps a lot!)

Two of the mid-day breaks are 90-120 minutes:

- Snack and nap.
- Walk my dog.
- Maybe run an errand: go to the post office, store, etc.

Evening Break

Of course, it's also important how we unwind, how much we sleep, and how we sleep.

Just like you can generate energy at will, you can also generate rest at will. This is what I tell myself when I am unwinding and getting ready to turn the lights off and sleep.

I've learned that I need to spend at least 7.5 hours lying in bed to feel fine the next day. Most of that time is asleep but even if I have minutes (or hours) where I'm not asleep, I still stay in bed: relaxing, breathing, thinking good thoughts (very slowly). I've learned that if I get up to do work or other things, I'll feel physically exhausted the next day.

Mid-Week Breaks

I like to work 6 days a week (Mon-Sat) because I enjoy my work and filling my time with impact-making activities.

However, I'm also aware of the need to take several mid-week breaks:

- Tuesday afternoon break is 4 hours long instead of 2 hours.
- Friday is two-thirds workday only.
- Sunday is no work at all.

During these breaks, I don't respond to any email or social media except for the occasional urgent thing, which I only allow a few minutes to respond, maybe a quick answer to say that I'll write more later.

Mid-Year Breaks

These are multi-day breaks off of work:

- February (Chinese New Year) we go visit my in-laws for a week.
- May is my wife's birthday and we take 2 weeks off, usually a trip.
- August is our anniversary and we take a few work days off.
- November is my birthday and we take a few work days off.
- Last 2 weeks of the year is holiday shut down, rest, extended family time, and reflection.

Stay Resting as Planned

Over time I've learned about how long I need to rest. So during breaks, whether it's a 15 minute nap or a 2-week break, I've learned to *stay resting even when I feel like getting up and working.*

I've learned not to trust my whims of working or resting in spurts, spontaneously... but instead, I find that if I work or rest in regular and consistent rhythms, I get a lot more done, and can maintain a healthy mind, body, and connection to Spirit.

To watch the companion video or comment on this chapter, go here: bit.ly/jpv2c21

22. The Importance of Keeping Appointments with Yourself

To give the accomplishment of your worthwhile tasks enough time (rather than doing things last minute), it's a good strategy to schedule multiple appointments with yourself to work on that project and make gradual progress.

This is how we build self-trust over time.

However, what if the appointment passes, and you didn't work on that project as planned?

You might:

1. Ignore the fact that you didn't work on it.

2. Blame yourself for having not worked on it.

Neither are healthy responses. I'll discuss each, then share my recommendations.

Ignoring your plan

Each time you plan to work on something, but ignore it when the time comes, you are practicing self-disrespect.

You know the project matters, and you planned to work on it at a specific time. It's a promise to yourself... which you then break. You wouldn't schedule with a client, and then just ignore the appointment, right?

This is essential to understand:

You are your most important client.

Nobody else's career, health, relationships, or spiritual growth, has a more significant effect on your ability to experience life to its fullest – to fulfill your mission, to serve the world with your unique and valuable gifts. You are your most important client.

The next time you schedule with yourself, remember this.

How you treat the promises to yourself – your own schedule – is either building your self-trust... or eroding it.

Make a decision that starting today, you will treat yourself like your most important client.

A quick thought experiment – bring to mind an important client in your business right now, someone you highly esteem. If you were making an appointment with them, you'd be thoughtful about their schedule, right? You would come up with a time that works for you both. And then you'd prepare (logistically as well as emotionally) for that appointment.

It's an important client, so you'll show up to give the best that you can, no matter how you were feeling right before the appointment.

Your own calendar is like the schedule of your most-esteemed client. Give it the respect it deserves.

Yes, you are welcome to reschedule with yourself if needed, but to cancel it again and again is highly disrespectful to your best client – and your sense of self-trust.

If you keep pushing back the work on that project, you'll either never do it, or you'll do it at the last minute, and thereby miss out on the benefits of gradually working on it and letting your subconscious develop the ideas over time.

So be careful not to schedule with yourself so casually.

This is why I'm such a big believer in using Focusmate to work on any important project, bit by bit over time. With Focusmate, I'm not only scheduling with myself, but someone else is also counting on me to be there.

Another common response:

Blaming yourself for failing to follow your calendar

The next time this happens, I encourage you to:

Be gentle.

Take some deep breaths.

Let's do another thought experiment – imagine that an important client has missed an appointment with you. They have sincerely apologized to you. Do you berate them? No, you would treat them with kindness. Then, together you would figure out how to schedule the next appointment at a time that is going to work better for them, to ensure they will definitely be able to attend.

Similarly, when you fail to follow your calendar – be gentle, forgiving, and then get curious. You are your most important client!

Don't ask self-blaming questions such as "Why am I so undisciplined?" Instead, ask *"What's something I can do differently next time, to make it more likely that I'll keep a self-made appointment?"*

Answers might include:

- Make your calendar more spacious – don't bunch up appointments and expect to be able to keep all of them. Put more buffer time between appointments.

- Schedule a shorter appointment to work on a tough project, so that it feels more doable. For example, schedule a 30-minute block, rather than a 2-hour block.

- For some projects it might work better to schedule a longer appointment: if 30 minutes feels futile for building momentum, a 2-hour appointment to work on the project might feel more doable to you.

- If you're feeling intimidated by the project, try starting your appointment with an energy/emotional-upliftment practice that works for you. I do what I call an energy reboot.

- At the beginning of the appointment, write down the doable steps for the project, so that you don't feel anxious about it. Then just calmly and joyfully start taking those baby steps.

If you keep missing appointments with yourself, this means you need to make each appointment a bigger deal: start with only 1 appointment with yourself per day. Or even just 1 weekly appointment with yourself to begin with.

Practice keeping that regular appointment with yourself, and then add more as you develop this muscle of keeping self-made appointments.

**

I used to not be good at this. And then I practiced, got curious, and practiced some more, using the techniques above. As a result, I now produce far more work than I used to, because I schedule time to do it, and keep to that schedule.

"I write only when inspiration strikes. Fortunately it strikes every morning at nine o'clock sharp." Somerset Maugham (one of the highest-paid authors of his era)

Ultimately, you need to be a student of your own energy and productivity. Learn how to schedule with yourself, and keep practicing and tweaking, until you are also able to be creative even within a schedule.

Be gentle on yourself always, yet continuously dedicated to the process of growth.

To watch the companion video or comment on this chapter, go here: bit.ly/jpv2c22

23. Step by Joyful Step to Your Success

If success were easy, everyone would be successful in their chosen field. Sadly, most people avoid much of the "hard" work needed to reach their vision.

Why is work seen as "hard"? It's usually because we intimidate ourselves. We imagine the entire project and how daunting it is. Or we try to take steps that are too big, and therefore, stretch ourselves too much, causing ourselves too much stress.

So when we meet resistance along the way, we turn to the easy stuff we already know, which aren't the things that are the most worthwhile. We keep delaying our most important work.

We don't realize that *we* are the ones stopping ourselves.

Yet here is the truth — step by step, we can get almost anywhere we want to go!

Nothing is too difficult, if you are willing to take the baby steps forward.

"Take the first step in faith. You don't have to see the whole staircase, just take the first step." —Martin Luther King, Jr.

For any project — no matter how large — you can always "chunk it down" to bite-sized pieces. The key is to keep moving forward.

An inspiring example is <u>Naveen Jain</u> — who has created a company that will take humans back to the moon in the next few years. He's not a rocket scientist. But step by step, he learned what was necessary. Step by step, he did the outreach to find the right connections to the needed technicians and financiers. Now, the moon is within his reach.

What is your moonshot? What vision really excites you?

Believe this: step by step, you can get to *your* moon, whatever your vision is.

However, don't just sit there dreaming about your "moon". Focus instead on the next doable step.

When you are tempted to give up, you've forgotten that step by step will get you there. You may simply need to rest a little while, and ask for support.

Consider these steps for achieving anything. . .

STEP 1. Write down your inspiring vision.

STEP 2. Brainstorm and write down the steps needed to get there. The steps don't have to be in order. They don't have to be accurate either. Simply write down the steps you understand now.

Why it's important to write down the steps instead of trying to remember them: The human brain naturally thinks about the obstacles and dangers to action. If you try to make progress without looking at a doable next step, it's easy to be scared of taking action. Write down the small, very doable steps and focus on each one.

STEP 3. Based on your current understanding, re-order the steps you've brainstormed and written down. What do you think needs to come first, second, third?

STEP 4. Now, notice if there is any large gap between the steps. Does any step scare you? That means you need to brainstorm smaller, more doable steps that can fill that gap.

A doable step doesn't take long to do, and is often a "visible" action. For example, "brainstorm ideas" is not visible, but "write down 3 ideas" is visible, as in, you can clearly see when you have done it.

Whenever you get stuck, you always have options...

- Go to a supportive online group and ask people what steps they would put into that gap. Be sure to give them context by sharing what steps you've already brainstormed. If you are shy, privately ask a friend or mentor.

- Give it a rest and come back in a little while, and you'll be surprised that you have new / better ideas than before. This is your brain's "diffused mode" at work. Your subconscious mind is working on the problem while your conscious mind is doing other things.

- Or use both options above: post the question, then come back the next day to add your own ideas to the thread! That way, everybody who is interested in that topic can benefit from it.

STEP 5. Take the next doable step, knowing that as you take action, more clarity will be revealed.

Imagine that you're driving to another city. You don't focus your eyes on that distant city. Instead, you focus on the road in front of you. Similarly, by continuously doing the next doable step, you'll eventually complete your project.

As you take each step...

As you take each step, remember your higher Truth, and embody that as you move forward.

Mantras that help me:

"Step by Joyful Step..."

"Step by Gentle Step..."

"Love and Gratitude for this next Step..."

"I don't have to know what the right order is... as I take another step, more clarity will be revealed."

"Action creates momentum."

"Action creates confidence."

If you learn to enjoy each step, you make the work more fulfilling. Through enjoyment, you are more likely to keep taking the actions that get you all the way to the result... to *your* moon.

To watch the companion video or comment on this chapter, go here: bit.ly/jpv2c23

24. A Conscious Life Requires Reflection Time

"On a daily basis, I go from task to task, event to event, responding to the world's demands, reacting to urgencies, emails, and deadlines. I don't have any 'thinking time'... to reflect, to reconnect to my deeper purpose & motivation." –a reader wrote.

If that describes you, then this chapter is for you...

Schedule Self-Care First

When I schedule my calendar, self-care comes first:

- **Several times in each workday**, I take a 60–90 minute break, which can include a snack, dog walk, and always, a 15-20 minute nap. These breaks allow me to mentally process how I've spent my day thus far, and briefly consider the next thing I'm doing. I never work for more than a 2-hour chunk of time.

- **Frequent stretch breaks** while I'm working, at least every half hour. Moving the body moves the brain. It gives me a chance to do my energy reboot and return to the task more refreshed, with a clearer perspective.

- **4 times a year** I travel to see family, taking a few days off – except during pandemics! During these week-long breaks, I schedule no work meetings nor required tasks. This allows idle-mind time. Even the traveling itself (commute to airport, the plane ride) is uniquely beneficial for reflection & big-picture thinking.

Keep strong boundaries for self-care, remembering that only with a balanced and renewed self, are we capable of being effective in our lives and in helping others.

Your state is your top priority. From there, everything else can be accomplished and done with higher quality. Get into your beautiful state of being first.

Ways of doing Reflection Time

Here are some times that you can reserve for reflection:

Puttering around the house

- Walking around the neighborhood

- Having a special long dinner date with You

- Booking an overnight stay at an airBNB or hotel (personal retreat)

- Going for a long bike ride, bus or car ride and talking with Yourself

- Taking a trip to the lake, ocean, forest, hills, mountains, or the desert

- Plan at least 1 day per month with no appointments, neither work nor social

- Be intentional about your commutes: reflect, reconnect & free-think

- Be intentional when you travel: don't schedule work requirements

- *(Do you have another activity/time that helps you to reflect?)*

What would you like to commit to? Intentionality is key.

Schedule it into your calendar / block it off so others can't demand your time.

Tell anyone who will be affected: co-workers, clients, coach, family and friends. Let them support you in keeping your reflection time sacred.

Questions for Reflection

Be intentional about the time you've set aside for reflection, rather than just letting your mind wander, which can sometimes be eaten up by negative thoughts.

Here are some questions — pick any one of them. After considering that question for a few minutes (talking out loud if it helps), be silent and allow your mind to wander into possible answers...

1. What am I here to do?

2. What is my Calling?

3. How do I best help others?

4. What is the higher purpose of my work?

5. How can I most effectively contribute to the world?

6. How is the world changing, and what can I do to adapt?

7. What topic do I love talking about, even when I'm tired?

8. What kind of person can I best help?

9. What project would I absolutely love to do?

10. If I had 1 year left to live, what project **must** I do?

11. What's stopping me? And what can I do about that?

12. Whom can I ask for help? What shall I say to them?

13. What is Universe / Spirit / God saying to me at this time in my life?

14. What is the purpose of my life?

15. What will energize me deeply?

During or after your reflection time, be sure to capture your thoughts. It can be in a journal, or with your phone's memo app.

Now it's your turn: Put this into practice!

The world needs you to be your most renewed and creative self.

If you've read this far, your spirit is probably asking you to have more (and better) reflection time...

To watch the companion video or comment on this chapter, go here: www.bit.ly/jpv2c24

25. Layer a Higher Meaning onto Each Moment of Work

What's stopping you from showing up fully for your work?

Oftentimes, it's not more knowledge, training, or ideas. The greatest obstacle I've seen in people is fear:

Fear of making a mistake... looking bad to others... disappointing yourself... fear of rejection... discouragement... tedious work.

Consider this mistaken perspective that causes the fear:

You believe that *the result* matters a lot.

It occupies a lot of your energy.

You think that the moment is all about the project you're working on... and therefore, your focus becomes attached to the results.

Consider this alternative...

In every moment of work, there's a much higher (or deeper) meaning.

Perhaps the truest meaning of this moment is not whether you get "good" results... or whether you'll have it easy... or whether you'll look good.

What the deeper meaning is, will depend on your life philosophy. There are multiple good answers.

How would you respond to this question:

"What is the higher meaning of each moment, that is more important than what's apparent on the surface?"

Here are 3 different philosophies.

I'd love to know which one you resonate with.

Philosophy 1: GOD

Imagine that you have the most loving and wise parent in the universe.

God is unconditionally loving, omnisciently wise... and happens to be your real parent!

God wants you to experience the deepest joy in this moment... in every moment... abiding joy and love... even when you are working on "hard" or "tedious" or "scary" work.

No matter what, however well or "badly" you live life, you are *always* loved.

You are a child of GOD.

You are completely protected in spirit. Your destiny is Heaven, and there is no possibility of you screwing that up! God's got your back completely.

Sure, you may take a longer and more winding road... but the protection and presence of God is available to you in every moment of your journey.

No matter the task, there is always the possibility of experiencing a higher joy... a deeper peace... an all-pervasive love that can change everything for you.

Every day, be willing to reconnect and to stay open to Spirit. Each day, be willing and open to experience God, whether a little or a lot!

Philosophy 2: Soul Evolution

You are here on Earth School to evolve your consciousness, your soul.

The stuff you do, the tasks on your to-do list, no matter how "important" or "urgent", matters far less than the opportunity each moment offers for your soul's growth.

Your calling is to be willing in every moment to notice what soul growth opportunity is available. To be open to that experience, whatever it may be.

There is profound and unlimited hope for you, and every other soul, because we are on an inevitable path toward greater wisdom, love, and creativity.

It's impossible to screw it up. Your destiny is protected and guided. Simply stay open and willing, no matter the task or experience in front of you.

You are always on a path of growth towards ultimate goodness.

Philosophy 3: YOLO

You Only Live Once.

Who knows what happens afterwards?

In this life, results aren't guaranteed, no matter how hard or "smart" you work. So you might as well enjoy the journey!

What's the point of suffering through tasks, or being afraid of them? You may get a "good" result one day, yet on another day the exact same action might create a "bad" result...

The more you live, the more you realize that there are too many factors outside your control.

Change happens rapidly in society, technology, the market, and even in your own biology. It's impossible to accurately predict the results you'll get. So relax within yourself, ok?

What can you *reliably* count on? It's only this: that you always have a choice — in every moment — to keep returning to a mindful calm and joy.

Think about it:

Nothing truly matters in life, that you can actually control, *except* your personal response to each moment.

Sure, you'll want to keep doing tasks that increase the *probability* of achieving future "goals"... but along the way, why not practice mindful happiness?

Whichever viewpoint you adopt, the core message is unanimous:

The higher meaning of each moment is joy.

It's not the email newsletter you have to write; it's not the webpage you have to make perfect; it's not the course you have to create; it's not the scary presentation to prepare for; it's not the tedious administrative work to get through.

The meaning that can be experienced in any task, in every moment, is the joy that is available.

Because it is of such supreme importance, the purpose of each moment is to first, and foremost, bring that higher state of being into your awareness.

Your state of being is your top priority.

Which of the 3 philosophies above resonate with you? I encourage you to write it down.

Or, write your own.

Then sincerely reflect on it regularly.

Look at it before you start your workday, so that you can keep practicing returning to the higher meaning within each day.

You might occasionally revise your written philosophy. Keep it fresh. Try different ways of rephrasing your Truth. Describe it in a way that helps you to reconnect to the greatest meaning of every moment.

The higher context I see for every piece of "hard" work that I'm faced with is to practice reconnecting with my core philosophy, and therefore, bringing gratitude, trust, and joy into this moment.

I frequently do <u>my energy reboot</u> to replace any negativity with positivity. I touch my heart, and I smile :)

Layer your "highest work" — the effort of bringing higher meaning — onto everything you do.

It's *not* about that project in front of you.

The higher meaning of this moment has a far greater importance.

Any task, any moment, can therefore be deeply enjoyed.

To watch the companion video or comment on this chapter, go here: bit.ly/jpv2c25

Acknowledgements

Six of my clients read the manuscript and gave me thoughtful feedback:

Brigitte Gemme – veganfamilykitchen.com
Faith Teo – faithteo.co
Jeffrey Scott – joyomancy.com
Leah Cooper – thecentreofki.com.au
Mojca Henigman – mojcahenigman.com
Pam Sourelis – wingedhorsewritingstudio.com

Book cover was designed by Mojca Henigman.

Thank you all!

To all of my clients: I honor your dedication to your deep and meaningful work, and your willingness to keep growing to become more effective as a business owner and human being.

To my workshop participants: Thank you for your sincere engagement with the material, and your thoughtful questions. You are helping me create better courses to serve all my students.

To those who watch my videos and read my posts: Each time I see your views, likes and comments, it encourages me, and inspires me to create better content. Your questions and comments have helped to make the content of this book.

To my referral partners: I'm deeply grateful for your trust in my ability to help those you send to me. I'll continue to do my best to make you proud.

Lastly, to my wife: My heartfelt gratitude for your loyal support and love!

About The Author

Since 2009, George Kao has been a marketing mentor, consultant, and coach to small business owners, speakers, and authors.

Georges mission is to raise the marketing effectiveness (and joyful productivity!) of those who prioritize integrity, compassion, and generosity in their business.

George teaches online courses about authentic online marketing, including advertising, authentic content creation, defining your core message, how to create and market courses, and joyful productivity. You can find all his current courses at www.GeorgeKao.com/Workshops

To receive a regular email newsletter with Georges best articles, visit www.GeorgeKao.com/Newsletter

Printed in Great Britain
by Amazon

26022365R00091